STREAMS
of Grace

May God's Grace
Rest Upon You!

Sam Wilder
7/9/20

STREAMS

of *Grace*

Where the Mind and Heart Are Free to Wonder

SAM WILDER

XULON PRESS ELITE

Xulon Press
2301 Lucien Way #415
Maitland, FL 32751
407.339.4217
www.xulonpress.com

EXULON
ELITE

Unless otherwise indicated, Scripture quotations taken from the New King James Version (NKJV). Copyright © 1982 by Thomas Nelson, Inc. Used by permission. All rights reserved.

Scripture quotations taken from The Message (MSG). Copyright © 1993, 1994, 1995, 1996, 2000, 2001, 2002. Used by permission of NavPress Publishing Group. Used by permission. All rights reserved.

Scripture quotations taken from the Contemporary English Version (CEV). Copyright © 1995 American Bible Society. Used by permission. All rights reserved.

Scripture taken from the HOLY BIBLE, TODAY'S NEW INTERNATIONAL VERSION®. TNIV®. Copyright © 2001, 2005 by International Bible Society. Used by permission of Zondervan. All rights reserved worldwide.

Scripture quotations taken from the Common English Bible® (CEB) Copyright © 2010, 2011 by Common English Bible.™ Used by permission. All rights reserved worldwide.

Scripture quotations taken from the Holy Bible, New International Version (NIV). Copyright © 1973, 1978, 1984, 2011 by Biblica, Inc.™. Used by permission. All rights reserved.

Paperback ISBN-13: 978-1-6312-9447-1
Ebook ISBN-13: 978-1-6312-9448-8

—————⧓—————

To my family and friends,
you have been unwavering in your support,
encouragement, and forgiveness,
and God has used you as a visible
and tangible expression of His love and grace.

CONTENTS

INTRODUCTION

"Preacher, you need to understand that your life is a symphony in the works. Its measures are being written on the pages of your days, and the greatness of your life isn't measured by wealth or position but by this single question: Has the melody of my life caused the world to dance?"

Having been in the ministry for over thirty years, serving as a pastor, evangelist, missionary, and Christian school administrator, I've had the incredible opportunity to meet some truly amazing people. One of those individuals was Mr. Jesse. I called him the music man. Mr. Jesse loved music. He loved playing it, and he loved listening to it. He played the banjo, the musical saw, and the piano. It was a joy to sit and listen to him play and hear him sing.

I enjoyed just being around him. He could make me smile no matter what my circumstances might be. Mr. Jesse was one of those individuals that make life better. You couldn't be around him very long before you felt lighter and more at ease. Mr. Jesse made the world around him want to dance, not because of his musical talent, but rather it was because of his passion for life itself. It was his quest for knowledge, his love of others, his humor, his ability to make one laugh when life wasn't so laughable. He made me want to be a better man!

I believe Mr. Jesse's contagious joy was an outflow of a heart full of love. He often said, "Love is the music of heaven itself, and the life that is filled with love is a melody that the world cannot resist." He almost always told me as I was leaving, "Preacher, go play heaven's song and help make the world want to dance!"

In this book, you will encounter God's extraordinary grace as you reflect on the stories of God being present in the ordinary, everyday stuff of life. If you listen to what you read, you will hear "Heaven's Song," and you will experience the melody of God's love and soon find yourself dancing in refreshing streams of God's life-changing grace!

The reflections in the book consist of events experienced by myself and others. You will find along the way inspiring quotes that will cause you to ponder and will conclude with a prayer point that will help in initiating a period of prayer. Following each reflection, there is an opportunity to dig deeper as you engage in thoughtful moments, assisted by questions that may help in better understanding the Scripture, and applying it in your life.

1

A PLACE CALLED HOPE

———✕———

*"Now hope does not disappoint, because the love of God
has been poured out in our hearts by the Holy Spirit,
who has been given to us" (Rom. 5:5).*

Have you ever been to a place so incredibly beautiful that
it takes your breath away, a place so spectacular that you
never want to leave? I've been to a lot of different places in the
world. I've been to Prayer Mountain in Soul, South Korea. I've
been to the wondrous countryside of Holland and strolled through
the flower market in Amsterdam. I stood at the River Jordan; I've
looked across the Plain of Jezreel and there, in the distance, viewed
Mount Tabor. I've stood atop the Fortress Mount near Megiddo
and looked out across the Valley of Megiddo, where the final battle
will take place. I've ridden upon the Sea of Galilee and received
Holy Communion. I've been to Kenya and Tanzania, Thailand and
South Vietnam, Costa Rica, and Honduras. The list goes on and on.

None of these places, as beautiful as they are, come close to that
place called hope. It is a place that one can only find deep within. It
is a place of encouragement, freedom, celebration, peace, expectancy,

and love! This place called hope is in sharp contrast to another site, a dreadful place, a place called hopelessness.

Hopelessness is a place that drains one of joy, peace, and ultimately of life itself. Many have traveled there—myself included. The good news is that one does not have to reside in such a place!

Hope, real hope can't be found in a particular location or situation, but rather, one finds it in the person of Jesus Christ!

———————◯∕✕———————

Prayer Point
Lord God, I pray today that I would experience the joy, peace, and life that comes from You.

WONDERING MOMENTS/QUESTIONS TO PONDER
(Read Romans 5:5.)

————————⊰✕⊱————————

1. When you hear the word *hope*, what images come to mind?

_____

_____

_____

_____

_____

2. Can you remember a time of experiencing hope?

_____

_____

_____

_____

_____

3. When you hear the word *hopelessness*, what images come to mind?

_____

_____

_____

_____

_____

4. According to Romans 5:5, what is the source of our hope?

_____

_____

_____

_____

_____

5. What is the reason for hopelessness?

_____

_____

_____

_____

_____

2

STEP OUT FROM
BEHIND THE WALLS

———◁——

*"I know that nothing is better for them than to rejoice
and to do good in their lives" (Eccles. 3:12).*

In his book, *Turning Hurts into Halos and Scars into Stars*, Dr.
Schuller begins by asking the question, "Are you hurting?" He
states that "Hurts are normal and natural—we can all expect them"
(Schuller, 1999). He shares the story of when he was part of a fif-
teen-member presidential delegation representing the United States
at the funeral of Mother Teresa in Calcutta. While there, they vis-
ited the orphanage that had been her life's work. He noticed while
visiting a framed poem hanging on the wall in the front lobby. The
poem entitled, "Anyway," read:

> People are unreasonable, illogical, self-centered
> ... love them anyway. If you do good, people will
> accuse you of selfish, ulterior motives ... do good
> anyway. If you are successful, you win false friends
> and true enemies ... be successful anyway. The good
> you do today may be forgotten tomorrow ... do good

anyway. Honesty and frankness will make you vulnerable ... be honest and frank anyway. What you spend years building may be destroyed overnight ... build anyway. People really need help but may attack you if you try to help ... help people anyway. If you give the World the best you have, you may get kicked in the teeth ... but give the World the best you have ... Anyway. (Schuller, 1999).

I believe that each of us has a choice. We can allow ourselves to become vulnerable and risk being hurt and disappointed by others, or we can withdraw behind the walls of isolation to protect ourselves from the pain of human interaction.

I admit the first is terrifying, but the alternative is nothing short of tragic. We cannot control how someone may respond to our well-intentioned actions, but through the indwelling presence of the Holy Spirit, we can face whatever comes our way, and we can do so with great joy and fulfillment.

———————⋈———————

Prayer Point
Lord God, may I engage those around me with a sense of expectancy and anticipation of all You will do through me as I give myself in love to others.

WONDERING MOMENTS/QUESTIONS TO PONDER
(Read Ecclesiastes 3:12.)

———————⋈———————

1. The writer of Ecclesiastes says that nothing is better for one's life than to rejoice. What do you think is meant by the term *rejoice*?

_____

_____

_____

_____

_____

2. What keeps a person from rejoicing?

_____

_____

_____

_____

3. The writer speaks of doing good. Is it always easy to do good, or do you find it difficult at times, and why?

_____

_____

_____

_____

_____

4. Are there dangers in isolating yourself from others, and if so, what might they be?

_____

_____

_____

_____

_____

5. While we can't control the actions of others, we can control our own? But how?

_____

_____

_____

_____

_____

3

SET YOUR GAZE UPON GOD

———————∝———————

"For I know the thoughts that I think toward you, says the Lord, thoughts of peace and not evil, to give you a future and a hope" (Jer. 29:11).

The late Peter Marshall, former chaplain of the United States Senate and author, once stated, "God will not permit any troubles to come upon us unless He has a specific plan by which great blessing can come out of the difficulty." (Schuller, 1999).

So often I am guilty of allowing the little things and, yes, the not-so-little things, to become more than they are. I find myself viewing life through the lens of my physical eyesight rather than seeing it through the lens of faith. And as a result, I become self-absorbed and miss the blessing God intended to be mine as a result of that particular difficulty or trouble.

Every day we have the choice to set our gaze upon God, remembering His sovereignty, or we seek to live life ignoring His plan and rely upon our self to overcome whatever difficulty or trouble we face. It has been my experience that when I set my gaze on God, my days seem filled with blessing, but when I seek to live apart from Him—not so much. God has a plan for your life and mine, and it is *good*!

———————◇———————

Prayer Point
*Lord God, I bow to Your sovereignty—knowing
that Your plans for my life are good. So, Lord, help
me to keep my eyes set upon You!*

WONDERING MOMENTS/QUESTIONS TO PONDER
(Read Jeremiah 29:11.)

———————⟨×⟩———————

1. How does it make you feel to know that God thinks about you?

_____

_____

_____

_____

_____

2. His thoughts for you are of peace and not evil. How does that square with your present circumstances?

_____

_____

_____

_____

_____

3. Jeremiah says God desires to give us a future and a hope. Describe what you see as your future.

_____

_____

_____

_____

_____

4. What hinders you from experiencing that future?

_____

_____

_____

_____

5. What steps do you need to take to realize God's plan for your life?

_____

_____

_____

_____

_____

4

STOP POUTING AND START OVERCOMING

———————∝———————

"Then he said to them, 'Go your way, eat the fat,
drink the sweet, and send portions to those for whom
nothing is prepared; for this day is holy to our Lord.
Do not sorrow for the joy of the Lord is your strength'"
(Neh. 8:10).

Helen Keller, writing about happiness in the face of suffering, wrote, "Most people measure their happiness in terms of physical pleasure and possessions. If happiness is to be so measured, I who cannot hear or see have every reason to sit in a corner with folded hands and weep. But as sinners sometimes stand up in a meeting to testify to the goodness of God, so one who is called afflicted may rise up in gladness to testify to His goodness."

She goes on to say, "The struggle of life is one of our greatest blessings. It makes us patient, sensitive, and Christlike. It teaches us that although the World is full of suffering, it is also full of the overcoming of it." (Schuller, 1999).

So, stop pouting and in Christ start overcoming!

————————✗————————

Prayer Point
Lord God, help me to stop pouting and in Your strength begin to overcome the struggles and difficulties I face with joy and gladness that comes from You!

WONDERING MOMENTS/QUESTIONS TO PONDER
(Read Nehemiah 8:10.)

—————⌒————

1. Life is not always easy, and at times it seems impossible. Have you ever experienced such moments? Name one of those moments.

_____

2. What has been your response in moments of great struggle?

_____

_____

_____

_____

_____

3. We are instructed to have joy, even in times of sorrow.

_____

_____

_____

_____

_____

4. What are some positive aspects of experiencing struggles in life?

_____

_____

_____

_____

_____

5. Where does our strength come from in moments of sorrow, according to Nehemiah?

_____

_____

_____

_____

_____

5

IT'S YOUR CHOICE

———————⊰✗⊱———————

"And He said to me, 'My grace is sufficient for you for My strength is made perfect in weakness.' Therefore most gladly I will rather boast in my infirmities, that the power of Christ may rest upon me" (2 Cor. 12:9).

Dennis Byrd, former New York Jets defensive end and quadriplegic, wrote, "What better way to test a professional athlete than through his body? I could easily have been destroyed when I was paralyzed out on the football field. I was weak and vulnerable, but 2 Corinthians 12:9 says, 'My grace is sufficient for you. My strength is made perfect in weakness.'" (Schuller, 1999).

There are many different ways a person might be broken—physically, emotionally, or spiritually. It is how one responds to the brokenness that is the crucial thing. If we are not careful, we may just find ourselves on the sideline, watching life pass us by, rather than dare to remain engaged with it. It does not have to be that way!

When diagnosed with Parkinson's Disease in 2017 at the age of fifty-five, I felt defeated. My body ached, I was always tired, my hands seemed to shake all the time, I was unable to focus, and it was hard for me to say the words that were in my head. I was struggling.

My effectiveness as a pastor was not what it had been. Shortly after being diagnosed, I was evaluated by a neuropsychologist for cognitive issues. I remember Him asking me a straightforward question. "Mr. Wilder," he said, "do you have Parkinson's, or does Parkinson's have you? It is your choice!" I could let the diagnosis define my life, or I could live each day with expectancy and anticipation of God's grand plan for my life. It's how we respond to the unexpected and unwanted in our lives that matters.

So, whatever challenges you may be facing today do so in His grace and strength, and as a result, you will realize how very blessed you are!

—————————⊂×⊃—————————

Prayer Point
Lord God, help me to respond to adversity and
the challenges I face this day with an awareness of
Your grace and in so doing, see the blessing that
You have given me.

WONDERING MOMENTS/QUESTIONS TO PONDER
(2 Corinthians 12:9)

————————⋈————————

1. Suffering is often a part of the human experience. Have you experienced brokenness—physical, emotional, or spiritual?

_____

_____

_____

_____

_____

2. How did you respond when faced with the situations?

_____

_____

_____

_____

3. What do you think is meant by the phrase, "My grace is sufficient for you?"

_____

_____

_____

_____

_____

4. What is meant by, "My strength is made perfect in weakness?"

_____

_____

_____

_____

_____

5. Why is Paul glad to boast in his infirmities (weaknesses)?

_____

_____

_____

_____

_____

6

BITTER OR BETTER?

---◇---

"That you may be sons of your Father in heaven; for
He makes His sun rise on the evil and the good, and
sends rain on the just and the unjust" (Matt. 5:45).

I came across a quote not long ago. It deals with the issue of one's
response to disappointments. We often think that because we
are good and seek to do the right thing in almost every situation
so that we are or at least should be exempt from the tragic occur-
rences of life. I once preached a message entitled, "I'm a Christian
and Life Still Stinks." Have you ever felt that way but didn't dare
say such a thing? Stuff happens to all of us. It's part of living in a
fallen world. But, still, the question is: "Why do bad things happen
to good people?"

Here is the quote, "Why do bad things happen to good people,
is the wrong question, for there is no answer. The right question is,
'What happens to good people when bad things happen to them?'
The answer? They always become better people!" (Schullar, 1999).

We have a choice today. We can choose to become bitter because
of the negative things we experience in our lives. Or, we can decide
to become better people, using those negative experiences that may

be a part of our journey in life as a source of experiential knowledge that can help make the world a better place. How will you choose? Will you become bitter or better?

Prayer Point

Lord God, help me to see adversity as an opportunity. Keep me from growing bitter, and help me become better.

WONDERING MOMENTS/QUESTIONS TO PONDER
(Read Matthew 5:45.)

—————————⚬—————————

1. How do you react to the bad things that happen in your life?

_____

_____

_____

_____

_____

2. Why do you tend to react as you do?

_____

_____

_____

_____

3. Why do you think the way you respond to disappointments or hardships matter?

_____

_____

_____

_____

_____

4. How can you keep from growing bitter during challenging times?

_____

_____

_____

_____

5. What defines us as children of our Father in heaven?

_____

_____

_____

_____

_____

7

RESPONDING TO ADVERSITY

———————◇———————

"And we know that all things work together for good to those who love God, to those who are called according to His purpose" (Rom. 8:28).

J oni Eareckson Tada, author and disability advocate, once stated, "I'd rather be in this wheelchair with God than on my feet without Him. In heaven, I look forward to folding up my wheelchair, handing it to Jesus, and saying straight from the heart, 'Thanks, I needed that.'" (Schuller, 1999). I love that quote!

We often allow adversity to control our lives rather than trust God in difficult times and situations. Joni didn't permit a tragic accident in her life to control her future. That's not to say she didn't struggle with her circumstances—because she did. But Joni didn't stay negative and full of self-pity. She pressed on in faith, trusting her future to God, knowing that He is sovereign and had a plan for her life. Thousands have come to know Christ because of her witness. Joni could have entirely given up, but she didn't.

Being a Christian doesn't exempt that person from adversity. Adversity is a part of life, and it comes to each of us. The critical difference, I believe, is how a person responds to that adversity. Joni chose to press forward in faith and, as a result, has lived a beautiful life.

When adversity comes knocking at the door of your life and my life, how will we respond? Will we trust in God, or will we allow ourselves to be controlled by the challenges that confront us?

Prayer Point
Lord God, whatever challenges I may face in my life, I trust in You, knowing that You are sovereign, and by Your Spirit, I can overcome.

WONDERING MOMENTS/QUESTIONS TO PONDER
(Romans 8:28).

1. Paul states, "that all things work together for good." How do you feel about the phrase, "all things?"

_____

_____

_____

_____

_____

2. Is that promise for everyone? Read the verse carefully before answering?

_____

_____

_____

_____

_____

3. Do you think that being a Christian should exempt you from adversity? Why or why not?

_____

_____

_____

_____

_____

4. Joni said she would rather be in a wheelchair with God than on her feet without Him. What does that statement reveal about her understanding of a relationship with God?

_____

_____

_____

_____

5 What role does our response to adversity play in our quality of life?

_____

_____

_____

_____

8

ADVERSITY IS NOT YOUR ENEMY

————————∝————————

*"Therefore I remind you to stir up the gift of God
which is in you through the laying on of my hands"
(2 Tim. 1:6).*

Washington Irving, essayist, novelist, and historian of the late eighteenth century and the early nineteenth century wrote, "There is in every heart a spark of heavenly fire which lies dormant in broad daylight of prosperity, but which kindles up and beams and blazes in the dark hour of adversity." (Schuller, 1999).

It seems when things are going well and we are experiencing a period of great blessing in our lives, we become comfortable and somewhat complacent. We are satisfied to stay as we are, and if we are not careful, we come to that place where we simply exist rather than fully live.

Adversity, I believe, can be the stick that stirs the dying embers in our life and rekindles the passion for life we once had. It can be used by God to awaken us to new and exciting possibilities. Adversity is not the enemy. Complacency is!

———————✕———————

Prayer Point
Lord God, awaken me to all the possibilities that await me. Stir up in me a passion for life. Let me not grow complacent but with excitement live each day for Your glory!

WONDERING MOMENTS/QUESTIONS TO PONDER
(2 Timothy 1: 6.)

———————✕———————

1. What do you think Paul meant when he told Timothy to stir up the gift of God?

_____

_____

_____

_____

_____

2. When are you most in danger of growing complacent?

_____

_____

_____

_____

_____

3. In what ways can adversity act as a catalyst in our faith journey?

_____

_____

_____

_____

_____

4. Is there a difference in existing and living, and if so, what is it?

_____

_____

_____

_____

5. Name some things you can do to rekindle your passion for life in Christ.

_____

_____

_____

_____

_____

9

DON'T HESITATE

———————⊷———————

*"Therefore we also, since we are surrounded by so great
a cloud of witnesses, let us lay aside every weight and
the sin which so easily ensnares us, and let us run with
endurance the race that is before us" (Heb. 12:1).*

I read a quote recently by Robert Schuller that stated, "When God says, 'Go!' Put on your track shoes" (Sculler, 1986). I love that! Don't hesitate; just trust God and go.

I realize that is easier said than done. So many times, we are guilty of attributing to God those characteristics that are common to man. Because we may have been let down by others in our life, we tend to be suspicious of others—yes, even of God.

To protect ourselves from the hurt and disappointments that are part of the human dynamic in relationships, we tend to construct a wall around our true self to insulate ourselves from being hurt. But the truth is that in so doing, we cut ourselves off from the very thing we long for the most—authentic relationships with those around us. We were created to be relational. Our primary relationship is with God, but we experience God in and through those around us.

Experiencing authentic relationships demands, by its very nature, that we are ourselves authentic. Don't allow the shortcomings of others prevent you from trusting the very one who created you! God loves you, and nothing will change that truth. We can trust God!

So, take off your slippers, put on your running shoes, and finish the race that God has set before you. You won't be disappointed, I promise!

———————◇———————

Prayer Point
***Lord God, may I not hesitate, but may I be quick
to show Your love to those around me.***

WONDERING MOMENTS/QUESTIONS TO PONDER
(Hebrews 12:1)

1. What picture comes to your mind when you hear the phrase, "Surrounded by so great a cloud of witnesses?

_____

_____

_____

_____

_____

2. Are there things in your life that are weighing you down? Take a moment and write them down.

_____

_____

_____

_____

_____

3. The writer of Hebrews uses the term *ensnares*. What message is he seeking to convey?

_____

_____

_____

_____

_____

4. We are encouraged to run with endurance. What does the word *endurance* say about the journey of faith?

_____

_____

_____

_____

6. Each of us has a race to run. Can you run someone else's race? Can they run yours?

_____

_____

_____

_____

10

BE EXTRAORDINARY

———————◇———————

"But the fruit of the Spirit is love, joy, peace, longsuffering, kindness, goodness, faithfulness, gentleness, self-control. Against such, there is no law. And those who are Christ's have crucified the flesh with its passions and desires. If we live in the Spirit, let us also walk in the Spirit" (Gal. 5:22–25).

How we approach each new day makes all the difference in the world. We can begin the day believing that it is "the day the Lord has made" and give ourselves wholeheartedly to fulfilling our purpose in it, or we can see it as merely another day in which to survive. How we approach the day impacts the influence our lives have on those we encounter. And, yes, you have influence!

Mother Teresa once said, "There is a light in this World, a healing spirit more powerful than any darkness we may encounter. We sometimes lose sight of this force when there is suffering and too much pain. Then suddenly, the Spirit will emerge through the lives of ordinary people who hear a call and answer in extraordinary ways." (Schuller, 1999).

As Christians, the very presence of God dwells in us in the person of the Holy Spirit. Because of that indwelling presence in our lives, the world around us is brighter and better.

I encourage each of us to yield to what the Spirit of God is doing in our lives, and as we do, the world will be a bit brighter and better, and many will experience healing through you and me.

———————✕———————

Prayer Point
Lord God, I yield to Your sovereign reign in my life. Use me as an instrument of Your healing grace.

WONDERING MOMENTS/QUESTIONS TO PONDER
(Read Galatians 5:22–25.)

1. Notice that Paul is referring to the fruit of the Spirit. What is Paul saying by the use of the phrase "of the Spirit"?

_____

_____

_____

_____

_____

2. What do you think is meant by "Against such, there is no law"?

_____

_____

_____

_____

_____

3. What do you think is meant by "crucified the flesh"?

_____

_____

_____

_____

_____

4. What is meant by the term "walk in the Spirit"?

_____

_____

_____

_____

_____

11

DETERMINED TO ACHIEVE

———✕———

"Jesus said to him, 'If you can believe, all things are possible to him who believes'" (Mark 9:23).

I once read of a blind boy who paid his way to a master's degree at Northwestern University by taking notes on class lectures in the Braille system of shorthand, writing them out on a typewriter, and selling copies to his classmates who had keen eyes but weak ambition. Robert H. Lauer wrote, "Nothing worthwhile ever happens quickly and easily. You achieve only as you are determined to achieve, and as you keep at it until you have achieved." (Tanner, 1999).

This young blind boy was determined to achieve his goal; even in the face of tremendous odds, he realized that goal. We often take the easy road, like those who, rather than taking notes, bought his. You've heard it before, "Nothing worthwhile comes easily" The truth is that we live in a culture that tells us we can have what we want when we want without putting in the sweat equity. There is an attitude, among some, of being owed something by those who have succeeded in life. Guard against being counted among those who feel entitled.

Instead, become what Norman Vincent Peale called a "Possibilitarian." No matter how dark things might be, look up and see what can be! This young blind boy didn't allow his physical blindness to keep him from seeing his future. What is it that's preventing you from pursuing your dreams?

———————— ⋈ ————————

Prayer Point

Lord God, enable me to view life with the eyes of my heart. And in those moments when tempted to take the easy way, and settle for less than You desire for me, convict and enlighten me that I might look up and pursue all that You have for me.

WONDERING MOMENTS/QUESTIONS TO PONDER
(Read Mark 9:23.)

———————⋈———————

1. What is meant by the word *believe*?

_____

_____

_____

_____

_____

2. Why is belief such a powerful force?

_____

_____

_____

_____

_____

3. In the reading, there was the story of a blind boy who was determined to succeed, and he did. What did he do that enabled him to graduate from Northwestern University with a master's degree?

_____

_____

_____

_____

_____

4. How do you define the term, used by Norman Vincent Peale, "Possibilitarian"?

_____

_____

_____

_____

_____

5. Do you view yourself as a "Possibilitarian"? Why or why not?

_____

_____

_____

_____

_____

12

BECOME A SOURCE OF ENCOURAGEMENT

————⚬————

"Therefore encourage one another and build each other up, just as in fact you are doing" (1 Thess. 5:11, TNIV).

Wilma Rudolph, when speaking of her success in both the 1956 and 1960 Olympics Games, spoke of the influence her mother had on her. "My mother taught me very early to believe I could achieve any accomplishment I wanted to. The first was to walk without braces." (Schuller, 1999). As a child, Wilma Rudolph suffered from polio but went on to win a total of three gold medals in track as a sprinter. From childhood polio to Olympic gold, what was the key to her overcoming? It goes without question that her dedication and hard work were significant components of her success.

However, her mother refused to allow circumstances to stand in the way of success for her precious daughter. Her mother, by faith, saw her daughter walking without braces and would not relent from that "faith sight." Wilma caught sight of that faith and claimed it for herself, and not only did she walk without braces, but she also ran her way to Olympic gold! The words we say and the attitudes we display toward others matters! Are we encouragers or discouragers?

There are so many who need to be encouraged to dream big. People need to know that you believe they can achieve. I saw it recently and wrote it down: "Come to the edge, He said. It's dangerous there, I answered. Come to the edge, He said. It's risky. I might fall, I answered. Come to the edge. Trust me! Come to the edge, He said. So I did. And He pushed me! And I flew!"

God is continuously calling us to new horizons. Are we by our words and attitudes helping others to achieve, to soar to new heights, or are we guilty of clipping their wings and destroying their dreams?

Prayer Point
Lord God, may I be a source of encouragement rather than discouragement in the lives of those around me today. Lord, don't let me be guilty of destroying the dreams of those around me. In the power of Your Holy Spirit, make me an encourager!

WONDERING MOMENTS/QUESTIONS TO PONDER
(Read 1 Thessalonians 5:11.)

———————◇———————

1. What is meant by "build each other up"?

_____

_____

_____

_____

_____

2. Are you an encourager? If so, in what ways do you encourage others?

_____

_____

_____

_____

_____

3. Wilma Rudolph's story of going from her suffering from child-hood polio to four Olympic gold medals is inspiring. What was a significant factor in her success?

_____

_____

_____

_____

_____

4. Can you think of some reasons some people decide to settle for something less rather than go after God's best in their life?

_____

_____

_____

_____

5. Can you think of someone who has been a source of great encouragement in your life? Name them and then write a note to tell them thank you for the role they have played in your life.

_____

_____

_____

_____

13

AWARE OF HIS PRESENCE

———————— ∝ ————————

"Am I a God near at hand," says the Lord, "and not a
God afar off? Can anyone hide himself in secret places,
so I shall not see him?" says the Lord, "Do I not fill
heaven and earth?" says the Lord" (Jer. 23:23–24).

Basil, who lived during the mid-fourth century, wrote: "Troubles are usually the brooms and shovels that smooth the road to a good man's fortune, and many a man curses the rain that falls upon his head and knows not that it brings abundance to drive away hunger." (Tanner, 1999).

There are those days, and I'm sure you've had them when everything seems to be a struggle, and you just want to quit. I know that I have had such days, and the temptation just to give up has been strong. But I have found it to be true that it is in the face of struggle that I see God and seek His embrace.

There are times I quickly turn away from the struggle and, in so doing, miss the blessing that comes in being aware of God in the midst of the battle. There are lessons to be learned in the struggle, and if we move away too quickly, we may miss the opportunity that it offers to encounter and experience God's presence.

Don't get me wrong. I'm not advising anyone to go looking for trouble and hardship. Hardships will come your way soon enough. What I am saying is, don't be so quick to turn away from hard things. Take some time in those moments to seek the face of God and hear His voice of comfort and wisdom and then, and only then, move on.

Can you imagine living your life in what Dr. Dallas Willard, author of *Divine Conspiracy*, refers to as a "continual conscious awareness of God's presence in our lives?" (1998). Knowing that in both easy times and challenging times, His presence is a source of empowerment and strength.

———————⋈———————

Prayer Point
Lord God, may I, in knowing that You are sovereign, always seek You in both good times and bad times. Help me to hear Your voice and learn Your ways.

WONDERING MOMENTS/QUESTIONS TO PONDER
(Read Jeremiah 23:23–24.)

———————✄———————

1. Have there been times when you have experienced God being very near?

_____

_____

_____

_____

_____

2. Has there been a time when it seemed that God was far away?

_____

_____

_____

_____

_____

3. Jeremiah speaks of God's presence filling both heaven and Earth. What prevents people from experiencing His presence?

_____

_____

_____

_____

_____

4. What do you think it means to live in what Dallas Willard referred to as "A continual conscious awareness of God's presence?"

_____

_____

_____

_____

5. How different do you think life would be if you lived with such a keen awareness of His presence?

_____

_____

_____

_____

14

STRUTTING LIKE CHICKENS

———————∝———————

"Trust in the Lord with all your heart, and lean not on your own understanding. In all your ways acknowledge Him, and He will direct your paths" (Prov. 3:5–6).

Have you ever been guilty of comparing yourself to others—measuring your self-worth by their seeming success? I know I have. As a result, I have, at times, found myself living life with a sense of having not measured up, of being a failure.

Have you heard this quote by Zig Ziglar? "Your attitude determines your altitude." How an individual views life has a great deal to do with their satisfaction or dissatisfaction with life. If a person sees themselves as a failure, there is a strong probability that they won't soar as high as they could have in life—strutting like a chicken in the yard, rather than soaring to great heights like an eagle in the wild. Don't be afraid to fail. Failure can be the first step to great things.

Several years ago, I was meeting with a member of the church in his office. While there I notice a plaque hanging on the wall that was entitled, The Truth about Failure. I won't share the whole thing, but here are a few of those facts. "Failure doesn't mean you are a failure ... it does mean you haven't succeeded yet." Here's another one, "Failure doesn't mean you're disgraced ... it does mean you were willing to try." One more for good measure. "Failure doesn't mean God has abandoned you ... it does mean God has a better idea!" (Schuller, 1999).

―――――――――◇―――――――――

Prayer Point
Lord God, I pray that I won't allow the fear of failure to keep me in the yard when You have called me to soar among the clouds!

WONDERING MOMENTS/QUESTIONS TO PONDER
(Read Proverbs 3:5–6.)

———————◇———————

1. Can you name a season in your life or maybe a single event that you didn't understand, no matter how hard you tried?

    _____

    _____

    _____

    _____

    _____

2. What does it mean to you to "trust in the Lord with all your heart?"

    _____

    _____

    _____

    _____

    _____

3. What do you think is meant by the phrase, "Your attitude determines your altitude?"

    _____

_____

_____

_____

_____

4. What do you think is at the root of our fear of failure?

_____

_____

_____

_____

5. Do you feel as though God is directing your steps? Are you where God wants you to be?

_____

_____

_____

_____

_____

15

DO YOU THUD OR DO YOU SING?

———————⟶⟵———————

"Oh, sing to the Lord a new song! Sing to the Lord,
all the earth. Sing to the Lord, bless His name;
Proclaim the good news of His salvation from day to
day" (Ps. 96:1–2).

"Have you been thumped lately?" A question asked by the author, Max Lucado. "When a potter bakes a pot, he checks its solidity by pulling it out of the oven and thumping it. If it 'sings', it's ready. If it 'thuds', it's placed back in the oven." He goes on to say, "The character of a person is also checked by thumping." (Tanner, 1999).

Thumps are those things that irritate and inconvenience us. Lucado goes on to say that it is these thumps that "trigger the worst in us." By catching us off guard and flat-footed, we are ill-prepared and often become reactionary in the worst way. These inconveniences and irritations aren't the same as a crisis—but faced with enough of them, look out!

When the inconveniences and irritations of today come, how will we respond? Will we sing? Or, will we thud? It's a matter of the heart. Jesus said that out of the nature of the heart a man speaks

(Luke 6:56). There is nothing like a good thump to reveal what is really in our hearts.

I love this quote by Lucado: "The true character of a person is seen not in momentary heroics; it's in the thump-packed humdrum of day-to-day living." (Tanner, 1999).

So, when thumped, do you sing or do you thud? *I want to sing!*

———————◦∝◦———————

Prayer Point
Oh, Lord God, when the pressures of everyday life seem overwhelming, I pray that I would run to You singing!

WONDERING MOMENTS/QUESTIONS TO PONDER
(Read Psalm 96:1–2.)

———————⟨⟩———————

1. Do you get irritated quickly? What irritates you? Why?

_____

_____

_____

_____

_____

2. Do you think it matters how a person responds in moments of frustration? Why?

_____

_____

_____

_____

_____

3. Much of life is routine. What do you do to maintain a sense of joy in the stuff of your day-to-day living?

_____

_____

_____

_____

_____

16

HE'S ALWAYS ON MY MIND

———————∝———————

"Draw near to God and He will draw near to you.
Cleanse your hands, you sinners; and purify your
hearts, you double-minded" (James 4:8).

Dr. Charles Stanley, states, "Our intimacy with God—His highest priority for our lives—determines the impact of our lives." He says God wants to reproduce His life in and through our lives (2012). That can't happen by our efforts, as well-intentioned as they might be. God must reveal Himself to us, bringing us into an intimate relationship with Himself.

All of humanity, according to Dr. Stanley, has a direct relationship to God because of who God is (Stanley, 2012). He is the Creator, the Sovereign Ruler, and He is Sustainer of everything. We all have a relationship with Him because of who He is, and that relationship is either intimate or distant.

Yes! One can, indeed, be very religious and not be close to God. You go to church, read your Bible on occasion, and even give in financial support of the church. As crucial as those practices are, they do not constitute, in and of themselves, intimacy with God.

Having intimacy with God means He is always on your mind and involved in every decision you make. He is closer to you than your very breath. Don't just be religious; be intimate with God, and if you are, your life will impact those around you in the most profound ways.

------------∝------------

Prayer Point
Precious Lord, keep me from falling into mere religion and guide me into a deeper and more intimate relationship with You.

WONDERING MOMENTS/QUESTIONS TO PONDER
(Read James 4:8.)

———————⋈———————

1. What do you think is meant by drawing near to God?

   _____

   _____

   _____

   _____

   _____

2. What is meant by being "double-minded"?

   _____

   _____

   _____

   _____

   _____

3. Can a person be very religious and still not be close to God?

   _____

   _____

17

CONFIDENT OR COCKY?

---✕---

"In whom we have boldness and access with confidence
through faith in Him" (Eph. 3:12).

Have you ever heard the phrase, "He's so full of himself"? It is said about a person who is more than confident—the individual is "cocky." He talks a great game but seldom lives up to his boast.

I suppose that we have all been guilty of boasting at one time or another. In an attempt to impress someone or maybe to advance our position, our influence over another, we have "talked a good game," only to be embarrassed or worse—humiliated.

One of God's acts is to bring us to the end of ourselves. This idea of God bringing us to the end of ourselves, on the surface, sounds combative and selfish on the part of God. Why would God seek to do such a thing?

The answer, I believe, is found in two words: redemption and restoration. It is what some have termed "the divine paradox." It is in our dying to self that we truly live. And it is in yielding to God that we are set free! Set free to be fully human, free to be the man or woman God created us to be.

I want to be absolutely and utterly dependent on God because I know it will result in my becoming the person God created me to be.

———————◁✗▷———————

Prayer Point
Lord, do what You must to bring me into submission to that place where I am entirely dependent on You so I will be the man You have created me to be.

WONDERING MOMENTS/QUESTIONS TO PONDER
(Read Ephesians 3:12.)

—————————⟨×⟩—————————

1. Have you ever said this about someone or had this said about you, "He's/She's so full of himself/herself"?

_____

_____

_____

_____

_____

2. What is the difference between confidence and cockiness?

_____

_____

_____

_____

_____

3. Define in your own words the meaning of redemption and restoration.

_____

18

YOU AIN'T ALL THAT!

———————⟨✕⟩———————

"For I say, through the grace given to me, to everyone who is among you, not to think of himself more highly than he ought to think, but to think soberly, as God has dealt to each one a measure of faith" (Rom. 12:3).

You've heard the song, I'm sure, written by Mac Davis. It became an international hit in the spring of 1980. The song is entitled, "It's Hard to be Humble." And yes, it was one of my favorite country songs.

Dr. John Dickson, in his book, *Humilitas: A Lost Key to Life, Love, and Leadership*, writes, "The most influential and inspiring people are often marked by humility." He continues, "True greatness, in other words, frequently goes hand in hand with a virtue that on the face of it, might be thought to curb achievement and mute influence. In fact, I believe it does the opposite." He defines humility as being, "the noble choice to forego your status, deploy your resources, or use your influence for the good of others before yourself" (2011).

Humility then is more about how one treats another than how one thinks about one's self. So, how do we do it? How do we live a life of power and influence fueled by humility rather than self-exaltation? The answer, I believe, is we must come down from the "mountain top of self-aggrandizement" into the "valley of broken humanity" as yielded vessels of God—allowing the Holy Spirit to have His way in us! My journey begins by remembering what a coach once said to me, "Sam, you ain't all that!"

———————⟨✕⟩———————

Prayer Point
Lord God, may my life be marked by humility. Let me always put others and their needs before myself, and in so doing, may I bring glory and honor to Your name!

WONDERING MOMENTS/QUESTIONS TO PONDER
(Read Romans 12:3.)

———————✂———————

1. Humility is a crucial characteristic of servant leadership. How would you define humility?

_____

_____

_____

_____

_____

2. Why does Paul warn against thinking too highly of yourself?

_____

_____

_____

_____

_____

3. What are some of the ways you might demonstrate humility?

_____

_____

_____

_____

_____

19

EVEN ON MY WORST DAY!

———————∝———————

"There is no fear in love, but perfect love casts out fear,
because fear involves torment. But he who fears has
not been made perfect in love" (1 John 4:18).

I have heard it said: "The greatest mistake a person can make in life is to be continually fearing he will make one." It's true, fear of failure can be paralyzing. This fear of failure can, if yielded to, cause a person to give up on a dream before he has even begun to pursue the dream.

Why bother trying, he may ask. I won't get it right, so why even start? Fear of failing, fear of making a mistake, fear of what others might think, fear of—you fill in the blank—paralyzes him. Have you been there, felt that, said that? If so, you are not alone!

I've made many mistakes over the years, as a pastor, husband, father, son, and friend; the list is long and seems to grow larger almost every day. Even so, I face most days with a sense of hope and a belief that each new day holds an abundance of possibilities. I do so because of one singular and unwavering fact: God loves me, and He loves you too! "There is no room in love for fear. Well-formed love banishes fear" (1 John 4:18, The Message).

Overcoming a fear-filled life happens in knowing the love of God as a personal and continuous reality in your life. The truth, even on our worst day, *we are loved*! And that is *good news*!

———————✕———————

Prayer Point
Lord, You are my Rock and my Hiding Place, and in You will I put my trust. Perfect me in Your love so I may be set free to love as You love.

WONDERING MOMENTS/QUESTIONS TO PONDER
(Read 1 John 4:18.)

———————⊂✕⊃———————

1. According to John, there is no fear in love. What do you think John means?

   _____

   _____

   _____

   _____

2. Knowing that God loves you is a powerful and liberating truth! Why?

   _____

   _____

   _____

   _____

   _____

3. What is one of your greatest fears? And how might you overcome that fear?

   _____

_____

_____

_____

_____

20

BEING A TRUE FRIEND

———————⌈⌉———————

*"A friend is always a friend, and relatives are
born to share our troubles" (Prov. 17:17, CEV).*

I recently reread a book written by a dear friend, Missionary/
Evangelist Mike Ricker, entitled, *A Heart Aflame*. In that book,
he states that "Life is a journey filled with many joys and sorrows.
Those who handle life best learn to glean from their experiences
inspiration that can help carry them forward on their journey of
faith." I love a quote he shares from a plaque he once saw, "Friends
are angels who lift us to our feet when our wings have trouble
remembering how to fly" (2004).

He goes on to say that "We were created for partnership. It is
the purpose of God to extend grace to us through the love, forgiveness, and grace of others." While that is true, many are living their
lives behind the walls of isolation they have constructed to insulate
themselves from rejection and disappointment that is often a part of
life. Everyone needs someone with whom they can be who they are.

Life is not always easy. And at times, it can seem almost impossible. How blessed is the one who has found a true friend! I love
this anonymous quote on being a true friend: "A friend is one to

whom one may pour out all the contents of one's heart, chaff and grain together, knowing that the gentlest of hands will take and sift it, keep what is worth keeping and with a breath of kindness blow the rest away." (Ricker, 2004).

Do you have someone in your life like that? If not, why not? Are you trying to be strong when you need the freedom to be weak? Are you afraid of what someone may say or think if they knew what was in your heart?

I tell you, if you have a true friend, you are blessed! And I ask; Are you willing to be that true friend to someone else? God knows, we all need a true friend, and He has provided that friend—his name is *Jesus*.

———————⟨✕⟩———————

Prayer Point
Lord Jesus, thank you for being that faithful friend. Thank you for always being ready to listen, and thank you for loving me. In your love, help me be a true friend to those in need.

WONDERING MOMENTS/QUESTIONS TO PONDER
(Read Proverbs 17:17.)

1. Do you have a person in your life that you count as a true friend?

   _____

2. What are some dangers of living a life of total self-sufficiency?

   _____

   _____

   _____

   _____

3. How does knowing that God loves you and that His love is not based on performance affect your day-to-day life?

   _____

   _____

   _____

   _____

   _____

21

LET'S GO DANCING

———————⋈———————

"And God is able to make all grace abound toward you, that you, always having all sufficiency in all things, may have an abundance for every good work" *(2 Cor. 9:8).*

Thomas Merton—monk, writer, theologian, mystic, poet, social activist, and scholar of comparative religion, states, "No despair of ours can alter the reality of things, nor stain the joy of the cosmic dance, which is always there." (Rohr, 2019).

He believed that the universe was continually dancing to the music of God's grace. He found that nothing could interrupt nor halt this "comic dance of grace." While an individual may refuse to join in the dance or hear the music, the universe never stops dancing, and the music never stops sounding!

Simply put, God's grace cannot be silenced. His grace is always sounding, even toward those who refuse to dance. The human response does not control God's sovereign grace. We can choose to dance or not. We can hear the rhythm of His grace or cover our ears and stand in the corner of creation and watch as the universe continues to dance without us.

It doesn't matter what you look like while dancing! The important thing in each of our lives is that we dance. Our dancing may not be graceful. We may often be out of step, but the key is just to keep dancing!

The remarkable truth for me is that the music of God's unwavering mercy and grace toward us never stops. I may refuse at times to hear it, but the melody of divine grace continues.

———————⋈———————

Prayer Point
Lord of the Universe, help me to hear the melody of your grace and grant me the courage to dance and to keep on dancing, even when it is the last thing I want to do. Lord, when the world seems to be dancing to a different tune, let me continue dancing to the music of Your grace.

WONDERING MOMENTS/QUESTIONS TO PONDER
(Read 2 Corinthians 9:8.)

————————⋈————————

1. What does it mean to have "all grace abound"?

_____

_____

_____

_____

_____

2. Who is the source of that grace?

_____

_____

_____

_____

_____

3. Why is the abundance of grace given? For what purpose?

_____

_____

22

SPRING IS COMING

———————∝———————

"I would have lost heart unless I had believed that I would see the goodness of the Lord in the land of the living" (Ps. 27:13).

"They may cut down all the flowers, but they will not be able to stop spring from coming," were words of wisdom from an old pastor to a struggling young pastor.

Have you noticed that some people always seem to be negative? Everything can be going great, and then it happens: we come face to face with the negative attitudes of others.

I've often allowed the negative attitudes of others wreak havoc in the "garden of my soul"—cutting down the dreams and visions of my life. I've allowed it to happen because of the focus of my thoughts and having lost sight of my real destiny as a believer in Christ.

Adverse circumstances, events, and yes, negative people are a part of the Christian's journey. Still, the truth is that those circumstances, events, and individuals are unable to stop spring from coming!

So, when disappointments come, and the journey is not comfortable, and all seems gray and at times without beauty, *remember spring is coming*! The sun will shine again. The flowers will bloom, and life will be beautiful, of that I'm sure!

———————⟨⟩———————

Prayer Point

Lord, keep me from becoming negative. Help me always to see life through the lens of faith in You. Let me speak life and not death to those whom I meet.

WONDERING MOMENTS/QUESTIONS TO PONDER
(Read Psalm 27:13.)

———————◇———————

1. What kept the Psalmist from losing heart?

   _____

   _____

   _____

   _____

   _____

2. What does the phrase, "the goodness of the Lord" mean to you?

   _____

   _____

   _____

   _____

   _____

3. What do you understand the following statement to mean: "They may cut down the flowers, but they will not be able to keep spring from coming"?

_____

_____

_____

_____

_____

23

BE QUICK TO FORGIVE

———————————∝———————————

"... bearing with one another, and forgiving one another,
if anyone has a complaint against another; even as
Christ forgave you, so you also must do: (Col. 3:13).

The young pastor sat, wondering, what would the old pastor's lesson be today. He knew it would be good; it was always good but, at times, uncomfortable to hear. "Be willing to forgive; it is impossible to move forward under the weight of resentment. And at the same time, be ready to forgive yourself." Had he been reading my mail? How did he know, but then he always seemed to know. He continued, "Son, when you make a mistake, remember that failure is not failing; failure is not trying again." Oh, how great is the wisdom of a seasoned man of God.

There have been times in my life when I have allowed resentment for another, whom I perceive had wronged me, to consume my day and render me ineffective. How about you? Unforgiveness toward another is a dangerous endeavor.

Unforgiveness does several things. It has the power to set the direction of your attitude, often causing you to become more negative in your outlook on life. It drains you of energy. Like a tree strangled by vines, robbing it of vital nutrients, unforgiveness can cause your heart to become dark and lifeless.

Life doesn't stand still just because you are offended or hurt by another. Life isn't stagnant. It's always in motion. And, if we are not careful to guard our hearts, we will find life passing us by as we stand chained to the pole of resentment, unable to move forward in our lives.

Prayer Point

Oh Lord, may I be quick to forgive and move forward in a more positive direction in my life. May I not give the spirit of unforgiveness a foothold in my life. Purify my heart, oh Lord, so that in all life, I may glorify You.

WONDERING MOMENTS/QUESTIONS TO PONDER
(Read Colossians 3:13.)

———————⊰✕⊱———————

1. What does it mean to "bear another"?

   _____

   _____

   _____

   _____

   _____

2. We are instructed to forgive as Christ forgave us. How far-reaching is Christ's forgiveness (partial or total)?

   _____

   _____

   _____

   _____

   _____

6. What are some of the dangers of harboring a spirit of unforgiveness? Is there someone you need to forgive? If so, what's holding you back?

_____

_____

_____

_____

_____

24

ONLY YOU CAN BE YOU

———————⌀———————

"I will praise You, for I am fearfully and wonderfully made. Marvelous are Your works, and that my soul knows very well" (Ps 139:14).

The picture in his office was of a field of beautiful wildflowers that seemed to stretch for miles, and there in the distance was a small figure of a person you could barely even see. The caption at the bottom of the picture read, "You are valuable. You are not one in a million, but rather one in six billion people who inhabit this earth. Only you can be you." I love that!

There are days I'm sure when you may feel that you don't matter. We often spend so much energy and time trying to be the person that others would have us to be rather than being the person, "who is fearfully and wonderfully made by God" (Ps. 139:14). Eugene Peterson renders the verse this way in The Message: "Body and soul, I am marvelously made!"

Know today that you are of great value; you are priceless. God made you because the world needs you! *So relax, lighten up, enjoy the real you!*

———————◇———————

Prayer Point

Lord, keep me from the trap of trying to please everybody and be who others want me to be. Grant me boldness and confidence to be the person You have created me to be.

WONDERING MOMENTS/QUESTIONS TO PONDER
(Read Psalm 139:14.)

———————⟨✗⟩———————

1. The Psalmist tells us that we are "fearfully and wonderfully made." Do you believe that is true about you? And if not, why not?

_____

_____

_____

_____

2. The Psalmist indicates that each of us is unique; each of us is a masterpiece. Do you celebrate that truth, or do you find yourself trying to be someone you are not?

_____

_____

_____

_____

_____

3. God made you for a purpose! Do you believe that you have a God-given purpose? Why or why not?

_____

_____

_____

_____

_____

25

KNOWING IS NOT ENOUGH

———————— ✕ ————————

*"But be doers of the word, and not hearers only,
deceiving yourselves. For if anyone is a hearer of the
word and not a doer, he is like a man observing his
natural face in a mirror; for he observes himself, goes
away, and immediately forgets what kind of man he
was" (James 1:22–24).*

Do you like being evaluated? Well—sometimes yes at other
times no. For me, it depends on the results. On this particular day, I was being assessed; first by the training team at my
Parkinson's fitness program and then by the neuropsychologist.
Parkinson's has both motor and nonmotor effects. It is a progressive
neurological disorder that affects the brain—and there is no cure.

Call me crazy, and some do, but I thought I was doing well
overall during my fitness evaluation. But then I had to sit and stand
without the aid of my hands to help push me up from the chair. I
then attempted to walk to the pace of a metronome while turning
my head back and forth at the same speed. Sounds easy, right? I had
to walk a straight line—heel-toe, heel-toe. Let's just say I'm glad the
police weren't there! But what frustrated me the most was trying

to put these little pegs in these tiny holes on a board, while being timed; I thought, *Come on, Sam, how long does it take a person to put a round peg in a round hole?* I left feeling a bit frustrated.

When I arrived at my appointment with the neuropsychologist, I was not in the best of moods. I entered the office, and the doctor asked me the same question he always asks: "How are you doing?"

I responded as I always do: "I'm fine."

"Well," he said, "your expression and tone are saying something else." (My wife and others have told me that I don't have to say anything—my face says it all. And don't get me started on tone!)

The conversation continued with my often-repeated refrain—"I know, I know."

"Sam," the doctor said, "knowing is not enough, you must apply it. Being willing is not enough. You must do it."

As Christians, just knowing is not enough; just willing is not enough. We must live out our faith, even in our moments of frustrations because the world is watching and listening. When others look at you and me, what are they seeing? When others are listening, what are they hearing?

---⧓---

Prayer Point
Lord, help me to be a doer of Your Word and not a hearer only.

WONDERING MOMENTS/QUESTIONS TO PONDER
(Read James 1:22–24.)

———————⋈———————

1. "Don't just talk the talk; walk the walk." James says it this way, "Be doers of the Word and not hearers only." What does it mean to be a doer of the Word of God?

   _____

   _____

   _____

   _____

   _____

2. Why is knowing about God not enough?

   _____

   _____

   _____

   _____

   _____

3. Would you define yourself as a doer of the Word? Is there an area of your life that you know doesn't line up with God's Word? And what do you plan to do about it?

_____

_____

_____

_____

_____

26

BREATHE DEEPLY AND SAY HELLO

———————∽———————

"Then you will call upon Me and go and pray to Me,
and I will listen to you" (Jeremiah 29:12).

In the book, *Fresh Air*, pastor, and author Chris Hodges shares about "trading stale spiritual obligation for a life-altering, energizing, experience-it-everyday relationship with God" (2012).

One of the essential keys to such a relationship is authentic communication with God (i.e., prayer). So, how is your prayer life? For many, prayer is an afterthought—spotty at best and often done out of a sense of obligation rather than a desire to spend quality time with God. I love what Hodges writes concerning one's attitude toward prayer. He writes, "As much as we might think otherwise, enjoying prayer is not an oxymoron, like jumbo shrimp or icy hot!" (2012). Prayer for so many is something on a to-do list that we can check off and quickly move on to "more pressing matters." How sad!

Martin Luther King Jr. said, "To be a Christian without prayer is no more possible than to be alive without breathing." (Hodges, 2012). It's in prayer that the "fresh air" of God's presence is experienced. It is in our genuine communication with God that we find new strength and courage and peace. Prayer is not an obligation or duty, but rather, prayer is an essential part of the Christian's life.

If it's been a while since you spent any significant time in prayer, may I suggest that you just stop—breathe deeply, and say hello to God, letting the life-transforming conversation flow.

———————✕———————

Prayer Point
Lord, I pray for a life of prayer that's not rooted in obligation or duty but rather a passion for Your presence.

WONDERING MOMENTS/QUESTIONS TO PONDER
(Read Jeremiah 29:12.)

———————✗———————

1. On a scale of 1 to 5, with five being very important, how important is the role of prayer in your daily life?

_____

_____

_____

_____

_____

2. What is your motivation for praying?

_____

_____

_____

_____

_____

3. Prayer is communication with God, and genuine communication involves listening. When you pray, does it include a period of listening?

_____

_____

_____

_____

_____

27

DON'T JUST TALK ABOUT IT

———————⚭———————

"Watch and pray, lest you enter into temptation. The spirit indeed is willing, but the flesh is weak" (Matthew 26:41).

Maybe you're familiar with this prayer, and you may have even prayed it or something like it. It's a prayer one prays when first waking up in the morning before getting out of bed. "Dear Lord, so far today I'm doing all right. I haven't gossiped, lost my temper, been greedy, grump, nasty, selfish, or self-indulgent. I have not whined, cursed, or eaten too much chocolate. However, I'm going to get out of bed in a few minutes, and I will need a lot more help after that. Amen."

Pastor Chris Hodges states, "When we begin each day by communication with our father, then we're going to feel a whole lot more connected to Him" (2012). Getting our hearts and minds right before we start our day is essential to living a life that glorifies God. Do note, however, that one prayer in the morning isn't going to cut it when confronted with the everyday stuff of life in a fallen world. We need to continue our conversation with God throughout the day. "We can't determine what happens to us, but we can determine what happens in us." We need to live each moment with an awareness of God's presence. We do that as we, moment by moment, yield ourselves to Him. By doing so, we are empowered to live a life that reflects the character of a true Christian—one who doesn't just talk the talk but walks the walk.

I want to start, keep, and end each day in conversation with God. How about you? Let's stay focused on Him, and today will be a *great day*!

————————⋈————————

Prayer Point
Lord, help me to stay focused on You today. May all I do today bear witness to my faith in You.

WONDERING MOMENTS/QUESTIONS TO PONDER
(Read Matthew 26:41.)

———————◇———————

1. What does Jesus mean by "The flesh is weak"?

_____

_____

_____

_____

_____

2. Do you pray only in emergencies, or is prayer a part of your everyday life?

_____

_____

_____

_____

_____

3. What are some reasons starting your day with prayer is essential?

_____

_____

_____

_____

_____

28

TRIUMPHANT!

———————⟨∞⟩———————

"You will show me the path of life; In Your presence is fullness of joy; At Your right hand are pleasures forevermore" (Ps. 16:11).

He had been battling pancreatic cancer for some time. He now found himself without the strength to push himself up to sit. Short of a miracle, he would soon die, and he knew it—and he was okay with that. He was more confident in God's love for him than ever. There was no bitterness in his voice. He was at peace with God.

The young pastor, who was a student of the "Old Man," stood by the bed, listening intently as his mentor and friend began to speak. With a voice so weak that the young pastor could barely hear the words of the old man, "Son pray; Make prayer a habit. Minutes spent with God," he said. "Make the day profitable. . . . Hours spent with Him make life triumphant! Go now and be triumphant." The old pastor then looked at his young friend and said, "Today I can declare that my life has been and continues to be more than profitable; it has been triumphant. . . . Son, pray, always pray!"

The questions confronting me this morning are: Sam, are you living triumphantly? Is your day spent with a constant awareness of God's presence? Are you content with merely checking in with God occasionally, or do you live each moment alert and listening for His voice?

Triumphant living isn't about the miraculous; rather, it's about His presence in our lives and our response to His being present!

Prayer Point
Lord, help me not to settle for just getting by, but by Your presence in my life through the indwelling of Your Holy Spirit in me, cause me, Oh Lord, to be triumphant!

WONDERING MOMENTS/QUESTIONS TO PONDER
(Read Psalm 16:11.)

―――――――――∝―――――――――

1. The Psalmist says that in God's presence, there is fullness of joy. What is it about being in the presence of God that results in joy?

_____

_____

_____

_____

_____

2. Why do you think the old pastor told his young student to make prayer a habit?

_____

_____

_____

_____

_____

3. The old pastor spoke of living a triumphant life and attributed that life to time spent in prayer. How much time do you spend in prayer?

_____

_____

_____

_____

_____

29

JUST IMAGINE

———————◇———————

"Change your hearts and lives! Here comes the kingdom of heaven!" (Matt. 3:2, CEB).

Richard Rohr, in his book, *The Universal Christ*, quotes Elizabeth Barrett Browning while addressing the topic of "Original Goodness." Here's the quote, "Earth's crammed with heaven, And every common bush afire with God; But only he who sees takes off his shoes" (2019).

I like the idea of earth being crammed with heaven and for the one who can see everything common set ablaze with God's presence.

Just imagine, what your day would be like if amid everything you encountered, and I mean everything: you saw heaven—everything ordinary burning bright with the presence of God.

I have yet to experience such a day. But that doesn't change the reality of "Earth being crammed with Heaven; every common bush afire with God." The problem is with my vision, my spiritual eyesight. I do believe that heaven is all around us. I'm just not sure I want to see—why? Well, because such a vision demands a response that I am, too often, unwilling to make. To see life through such eyes would require of me the taking off my shoes of self-gratification and self-promotion, and while I have, in certain moments, done so, it seems I'm always putting them back on.

Today, it is my goal to go longer with my "shoes of self" removed than yesterday; and tomorrow even longer. Just imagine seeing heaven in our everyday lives. I think our lives would be different-better, more vibrant, and more complete!

———————✕———————

Prayer Point
Lord God, open the eyes of my heart so that I may see the reality of heaven all around me, and give me the courage to remove my shoes of self and keep me from putting them back on.

WONDERING MOMENTS/QUESTIONS TO PONDER
(Read Matthew 3:2.)

———————◦✕◦———————

1. What does Elizabeth Browning mean by, "Earth is crammed with heaven"?

_____

_____

_____

_____

_____

2. She states that "every common bush ablaze with God's presence." How can you be more aware of God being present in the ordinary things of life?

_____

_____

_____

_____

_____

3. Why do you think some are afraid to experience the presence of God in their everyday life?

_____

_____

_____

_____

_____

30

STOP THE NOISE

———————✄———————

"We love Him because He first loved us" (1 John 4:19).

"Love is a paradox," states Richard Rohr. "It often involves making a clear decision, but at its heart, it is not a matter of mind or willpower but a flow of energy willing allowed and exchanged without requiring payment in return" (2019).

To give love, without expectation of having the same given in return, is a divine thing. We often speak of such things as unconditional love, sacrificial love—yet seldom do we extend the same to others. Oh, we want to be the recipients of it, and we are in Christ!

Why is it that we are so hesitant to give love when we are so loved? Maybe we are unaware of being loved that way. Knowing the concept of divine love and being continually aware of it are not the same.

The world is a noisy place and can make it difficult to hear the "grand symphony" of God's love toward all humankind. But be assured that regardless of the world's noise, the symphony of God's love continues to play. Many hear the noise but deep within are longing to hear the music of God's love.

Our lives as believers should be as a symphony, yet sadly, we are guilty of making a lot of noise! It is my prayer that today I won't be so noisy, and as a result, someone will truly hear the music of God's "Amazing Grace."

Prayer Point
Lord God, keep me from adding to the noise of the world, and instead, let my life sing of Your love and grace.

WONDERING MOMENTS/QUESTIONS TO PONDER
(Read 1 John 4:19.)

———————⟨⟩———————

1. Why are we empowered to love others because we are aware that
    God loves us?

    _____

    _____

    _____

    _____

    _____

2. What is our human tendency when it comes to loving others?

    _____

    _____

    _____

    _____

    _____

3. Why are we often reluctant to love others even when God so loves us?

_____

_____

_____

_____

_____

31

I STILL STRUGGLE

———————⚮———————

"Cast all your anxiety on him because he cares for you"
(1 Peter 5:7, NIV).

D o you ever get anxious about anything? It's a silly question, I suppose. I'm sure we've all had moments when our concern about something or someone becomes more than mere concern— we are anxious.

For most, it is only a moment here and there; but for some, those moments become days and days that become weeks and weeks and then become months. I am one of those. I struggle with anxiety and depression almost daily. "Sam, you're a pastor; you shouldn't be anxious! The Bible says ..." Yes, I know what the Bible says, and I believe it, but I still struggle.

My greatest struggle comes in not feeling free to be authentic— maybe transparent is a better word—about my battle with anxiety and depression. I realize that by sharing this, I risk having some whisper questions about my faith. However, it is because of that faith that I can write about my struggle.

God has been good to me, and loving, and patient. It is in the struggle that I have desperately sought His presence. And, in doing so, I have always found God patiently waiting for me to give Him all of my anxiety. "The difficulties we face can't be our problems and God's problems at the same time. When we realize that He is in control, It's much easier to relax and enjoy the present moment (Hodges, *2012*).

---—◁✕▷—---

Prayer Point
Lord, help me to live each moment—keenly aware of Your presence with me and enable me to relax and enjoy each moment as I trust in You!

WONDERING MOMENTS/QUESTIONS TO PONDER
(Read 1 Peter 5:7.)

———————◁✕▷———————

1. What things make you anxious? Why?

_____

_____

_____

_____

_____

2. What is meant by "Cast all your anxiety on Him"?

_____

_____

_____

_____

_____

3. How would your life be different if you were continually aware of God being present with you?

_____

_____

_____

_____

_____

32

CONFRONTATIONAL PRAYER

———————✕———————

"Finally, my brethren, be strong in the Lord and in the power of His might. Put on the whole armor of God, that you may be able to stand against the wiles of the devil. For we do not wrestle against flesh and blood, but against principalities, against powers, against the rulers of the darkness of this age, against spiritual hosts of wickedness in heavenly places" (Eph. 6:10–12).

I had never seen nor had I ever heard anything like what I was seeing and hearing on that early morning in May of 1989 in the chapel at Kwang-Lim World Prayer Center in Seoul, South Korea. People were pacing back and forth and shouting. Some were crying, others were clapping, and still, others were shaking their fist. I just stood there confused and a bit unsettled. It was supposed to be an early morning prayer gathering. It looked more like a violent protest than a prayer meeting.

As I stood watching, a young woman walked up to me and in broken English asked if I were okay. I said I was even though I wasn't fine! She sensed my discomfort and confusion and began to share with me what was happening. They were indeed praying, but it wasn't the peaceful, meditative prayer to which I was accustomed. These prayer warriors, several hundred, had gathered for battle. They were engaging in "spiritual warfare." She began to interpret some of what was being said by those who were so fervently praying.

They were praying for God's kingdom to come on earth as it is in heaven. They were praying that the enemy of humanity would be silenced and that the whole earth would be filled with the goodness and love of God. As the young woman continued, I began to understand—there are times when *confrontational prayer* is necessary.

"Too often, we think of prayer as a pleasant, dreamy meditation, but sometimes our prayers should be more like a street fight" (Hodges, *2012*). Hodges continues by stating, "If you want to make a difference with your prayers, then you can't just think of prayer as a time to sit and meditate on happy thoughts for ten minutes." There are times when you and I need to confront the devil using the weapons God has given us. The Bible tells us in James 5:16, "The effectual fervent prayer of a righteous man availeth much."

When was the last time you prayed fervently? What is worth fighting for in your life? Don't get me wrong; I love my quiet time. But, there are times when confronted by the one who would seek to steal what God has given, that my quiet time need not be so calm!

———————⋈———————

Prayer Point
Lord, strengthen my prayer life. Help me to recognize those times when I need to stand and fight in prayer!

WONDERING MOMENTS/QUESTIONS TO PONDER
(Read Ephesians 6:10–12.)

———————⊰⊱———————

1. How would you define confrontational prayer?

    _____

    _____

    _____

    _____

    _____

2. Why should we put on the armor of God?

    _____

    _____

    _____

    _____

    _____

3. What is spiritual warfare, and why is it essential for the church
    to engage in it?

    _____

    _____

    _____

    _____

    _____

33

SELF-DENIAL

———————⋉———————

"When He had called the people to Himself, with His disciples also, He said to them, 'Whoever desires to come after Me, let him deny himself, and take up his cross, and follow Me'" (Mark 8:34).

The saying goes, "Flatter me, and I may not believe you. Criticize me, and I may not like you. Ignore me, and I may not forgive you. Encourage me, and I may not forget you." (Tanner, 1999).

I don't know about you, but I would rather be that person who encourages others. Encouragement is a beautiful gift that. when given, can cause the recipient to press on in times of great difficulty and not lose hope. Every day we encounter others who need to be encouraged, and when we do, we choose to offer that encouragement—or we don't.

Yet, we often miss the opportunity because we haven't the eyes to see the need. The reason we fail to see, I believe, is because we are so focused on ourselves and our own needs.

The greatest obstacle to our being an encouragement to others is ourselves. I've been told, more than once, "Sam, you need to get over yourself—the world doesn't revolve around you!" I know it's true, but still, the self seems to always get in the way. That's why I must continually put to death self and find life in Christ.

I have found that when I purposefully yield to the Lord, I become more aware of others and their needs and less focused on having others meet my wants. Becoming an encourager begins with self-denial.

———————— ⋊ ————————

Prayer Point
Lord, lead me to get over myself and see the needs of those around me, especially their need to be encouraged!

WONDERING MOMENTS/QUESTIONS TO PONDER
(Read Mark 8:34.)

———————⋈———————

1. What does it mean to deny self?

_____

_____

_____

_____

_____

2. What is meant by "take up your cross"?

_____

_____

_____

_____

_____

3. What is our most significant obstacle in becoming an encourager, and what can you do to overcome the obstacle?

_____

_____

_____

_____

_____

34

OUR RESPONSE MATTERS

———————∝———————

"These things I have spoken to you, that in Me you may have peace. In the world, you will have tribulation, but be of good cheer. I have overcome the world" *(John 16:33).*

All of us have our own set of problems. No one's life is free of challenges. It's a part of living in this world. It's not a question of if, but when. How do we respond when the unwanted and unexpected stare us down? It's an important question. It's important because how we respond bears witness to our faith or the lack of our faith.

"To welcome a problem without resentment is to cut its size in half ... Problems are challenges we can complain about, dwell on, give in to—or think through ... We can spend our time aimlessly licking our wounds or aggressively licking our problems ... Our goliaths can be feared or fought, succumbed to, or slain" (Ricker, 2004).

How we respond, when faced with problems, reveals the actual condition of our faith. Having faith doesn't mean that when life throws a punch at you, you aren't momentarily stunned or even knocked down. What it does mean is that when stunned, you shake it off, and when knocked down, you get up!

John Wesley said it best when he said, "The best of all, God is with us!"(Ricker, 2004).

———————⊂✕⊃———————

Prayer Point

Lord, when faced with problems, I respond with faith in You. May I remember that You are always with me, and Your Holy Spirit dwells in me. I am not alone in facing my problems. Help me, Lord, to trust You in every situation I face.

WONDERING MOMENTS/QUESTIONS TO PONDER
(Read John 16:33.)

———————◇———————

1. What is meant by "being in Christ"?

_____

_____

_____

_____

_____

2. We can have peace and joy in our lives, even amid the many conflicts in today's world. How is that made possible?

_____

_____

_____

_____

_____

3. Our response to problems reveals the actual condition of our faith. Why?

_____

_____

_____

_____

_____

35

WE ARE OUR OWN WORST ENEMY

———————✂———————

"Where do wars and fights come from among you? Do they not come from your desires for pleasure that war in your members? You list and do not have. You murder and covet and cannot obtain. You fight and war. Yet you do not have because you do not ask. You ask and do not receive, because you ask amiss, that you may spend it on your pleasures. Adulterers and adulteresses! Do you not know that friendship with the world is enmity with God? Whoever therefore wants to be a friend of the world makes himself an enemy of God. Or do you think that the Scripture says in vain, "The Spirit who dwells in us yearns jealously?" But He gives more grace. Therefore He says: "God resists the proud, But gives grace to the humble." (James 4:1–6)

I'm sure you've seen the acrostic H.A.L.T. It means one should avoid becoming too hungry, angry, lonely, or tired. The reason being that it is in those moments that we are in danger of making some poor decisions, and with every decision, there are consequences.

We are often guilty of blaming others for the adverse circumstances in our lives when the truth is, we are the cause of those circumstances. We have made poor choices. I know that I have made a lot of them. I've rushed when I should have waited. I've hesitated when I should have acted. I've talked when I should have been quiet and listened. I've been demanding when I should have been more understanding. Well, you get the idea.

In most cases, I am the cause of my troubles—not God or the devil or other people—and to be honest, that's a hard pill to swallow. You, too, have heard the saying: "We are our own worst enemy." I believe it!

The good news is that God's grace and mercy are not far from us. They are ever-present. They are nearer to us than our breath. So, just stop and breathe! Realize that in God, we find redemption and restoration. Even when we make poor choices that carry a hefty price, God does not reject us. He doesn't turn His back on us. God doesn't give up on us. He continues to believe in the goodness that dwells in all He has created—including you and me.

Today I want to stop; I want to H.A.L.T. and just breathe in God and exhale self. I want to yield to what the Holy Spirit is doing in my life. I want to encourage you to do the same.

———————⋈———————

Prayer Point

Lord, help me to realize that blaming others for my poor choices is unproductive, and is itself a poor choice. Lord, give me the courage to take responsibility for my actions. Help me make decisions that are in keeping with Your will for my life.

WONDERING MOMENTS/QUESTIONS TO PONDER
(Read James 4:1–6.)

————————<>————————

1. Why do you think we often blame others for the adverse circumstances in our lives?

———————————————————————————————

———————————————————————————————

———————————————————————————————

———————————————————————————————

2. What does the acrostic H.A.L.T. stand for, and why is it important?

———————————————————————————————

———————————————————————————————

———————————————————————————————

———————————————————————————————

3. How are we our own worst enemy, according to James 4:1–6?

_____

_____

_____

_____

_____

36

HIS HEART HAS BECOME MY PILLOW

————————⊰✦⊱————————

"And it shall come to pass in the last days, says God, that I will pour out of My Spirit on all flesh; Your sons and your daughters shall prophesy. Your young men shall see visions; your old men shall dream dreams" (Acts 2:17).

The following quote is from the book, *Mondays with My Old Pastor*: "Dream big dreams, and you will achieve great things, but make sure to dream using God's heart as a pillow" (Navajo, 2012).

I'm sure we've all had big dreams, and we may have even realized some of those dreams. The question is not, can we accomplish great things; the truth is we can achieve almost anything we set out to do. The real issue for me is—where do my dreams originate? Are they the result of ever-increasing intimacy with God, or are they nothing more than a portrait of a life characterized by self-centeredness?

Often our big dreams, while they may be admirable as seen by others, are not God's heartbeat for our lives. We wonder why we feel dissatisfied and unfulfilled, even though others would say we've been successful. Could it be that our dreams have come while resting upon the "pillow of this world" rather than God's heart?

So, for the one who dares to hear the heartbeat of God—know that what you hear may not be what you thought it would be. The dream may not be what you expected or what others expected from you. The question is, are you okay with that?

———————⟨×⟩———————

Prayer Point
Lord, may your heart be my pillow, and may the sound of Your heartbeat become the source of my dreams.

WONDERING MOMENTS/QUESTIONS TO PONDER
(Read Acts 2:17.)

————————⟨✕⟩————————

1. What does it mean that God will, in the last days, pour out His Spirit on all flesh?

_____

_____

_____

_____

_____

2. What do you think the phrase "Make sure to dream using God's heart as a pillow"?

_____

_____

_____

_____

_____

3. Why do you think so many people are dissatisfied with their life?

_____

_____

_____

_____

_____

37

LONGING TO CONNECT WITH OTHERS

—————◇—————

"Bear one another's burdens, and so fulfill the law of Christ" (Gal. 6:2).

To experience true friendship is liberating. Having someone with whom you can share honestly and genuinely is a treasure to be handled with care. C. S. Lewis states: "Friendship is born at the moment one person says to another, 'What! You, too? I thought I was the only one.'" Each of us needs others who will care enough to listen and understand us. Yet, for many, that need will go unmet because of past hurts and wounds. The world around us is full of wounded people who would rather live in loneliness than experience such pain again. Oh, we may not see them because of the masks they wear to hide their pain, but they are all around us. The unfortunate truth is that you and I may be sitting next to them in church and not even know it. Maybe you are that person.

The one place a person should find the courage to risk being their authentic self is in the community of faith—the church. God never meant for us to walk through life alone. And deep down, we know it. "A longing for connection, for friendship, for relationship is a foundational part of every human being" (Hodges, *2012*). People want to belong. They need to know they matter!

———————◇———————

Prayer Point
God, give Your church the courage to remove its
mask and risk connecting with hurting humanity!
And, Lord God, start with me!

WONDERING MOMENTS/QUESTIONS TO PONDER
(Read Galatians 6:2.)

———————✕———————

1. What are some of the ways you can bear the burdens of another person?

_____

_____

_____

_____

_____

2. Authentic friendship is liberating. Why?

_____

_____

_____

_____

_____

3. The community of faith is the one place where a person should find the courage to be authentic. Why do you think many feel they can't be honest and transparent in church about their struggles?

_____

_____

_____

_____

_____

38

YOUR FACE SAYS IT ALL

———————⟨✕⟩———————

"Out of the same mouth proceed blessing and cursing. My brethren, these things ought not to be so. Does a spring send forth fresh water and bitter from the same opening? Can a fig tree, my brethren, bear olives, or a grapevine bear figs? Thus no spring yields both saltwater and fresh" (James 3:10–12).

R. T. Kendall, in his book, *Controlling the Tongue*, states the obvious: "We will never be perfect in this life, But it doesn't mean we shouldn't try" (2007). What we say and how we say it matters! As Christian, our motivation to get life right, including how we speak, is our desire to be more like Christ. We want to please God more and more. Kendall states that while we are not perfect, we can indeed improve (2007). The real question is, do we want to improve or not?

Let's face it; sometimes it just feels good to tell that one person how you feel or what you are thinking! Trust me when I say that is not a good idea. And I've learned that I can say negative things without even uttering a word. It's true. I've been told on more than one occasion, "Sam, you don't have to say it; your face says it all!"

The world is listening. What are we saying, not only with our words but also with our actions? Now while we may not be perfect, we can be better. It was William Cowper who said, "I am not what I ought to be, not what I wish to be, I am not what I hope to be, not what I once was, but by the grace of God, I am what I am." (Kendall, 2007).

The tongue is a small but powerful thing. With it, we speak life or death. It is only by God's grace that we speak life to others. While we may not be perfect, we can and should improve. I want to be better today than yesterday and tomorrow better still. What we say and how we say it matters! In the words of my third-grade teacher, "Sammy, watch your mouth!" So, today I plan to do just that.

Prayer Point
Lord, guard my tongue and make it an instrument of Your life-giving grace to a broken and hurting world.

WONDERING MOMENTS/QUESTIONS TO PONDER
(Read James 3:10–12.)

————————⊂✕————————

1. Why does what we say and how we say it matter?

_____

_____

_____

_____

_____

2. Have you ever told somebody how you feel when those feelings were not favorable, and doing so made you feel good? Why do you think it made you feel good?

_____

_____

_____

_____

_____

3. The tongue, though small, is mighty. Why is it so powerful?

_____

_____

_____

_____

_____

39

IN HIS HANDS

———————⟡———————

"But we all, with unveiled face, beholding as in a mirror the glory of the Lord, are being transformed into the same image from glory to glory, just as by the Spirit of the Lord" (2 Cor. 3:18).

Maxie Dunnam tells the story about having received an extraordinary gift from a prisoner who was serving a life sentence with no chance of parole. Maxie had met the man only once while visiting the prison where the man was serving out his sentence. The one thing Maxie remembered about the man was how gifted he was in the art of sculpting wood.

After holding the package for several minutes wondering what it might be and why the man had sent him a gift, Maxie opened the box to find inside a beautiful set of praying hands that had been carved by the man. The wood looked as if it had been scorched by fire. Maxie had never seen anything quite like it.

Accompanying the carved hands was a handwritten note from the imprisoned artisan. The card read, "There is no life so stricken by tragedy or devastated by sin that it cannot be transformed into a beautiful thing when placed in the Master's hands!"

You see, the wood used to carve the set of praying hands came from a tree in the prison courtyard. The tree having been struck by lightning during a fierce thunderstorm, to the untrained eye, looked hopelessly dead. But this master craftsman, whose life had been transformed by the Good News of God's grace, saw within the tree an image of what God had done for him. His life, devastated by sin, had been transformed into a beautiful thing as he yielded his life to God. (Dunnam, 2010).

———————×———————

Prayer Point
Lord, I pray that You would create something beautiful of my life. May my life become a witness to Your glory and goodness. Lord, I pray for those I meet today, that they might see the wonder and beauty of Your presence in me and give You glory.

WONDERING MOMENTS/QUESTIONS TO PONDER
(Read 2 Cor. 3:18.)

—————————⌘—————————

1. Paul tells us that "we are being transformed into the same image from glory to glory by the Spirit of the Lord." Try and describe that image.

    _____

    _____

    _____

    _____

    _____

2. What did the set of praying hands, carved by the prisoner, represent?

    _____

    _____

    _____

    _____

    _____

3. Is there any life so devastated by sin that God can not transform it into a beautiful thing? Why or why not?

_____

_____

_____

_____

_____

40

BREAD CRUMBS

———— ⚬ ————

"Surely He shall deliver you from the snare of the fowler, and from the perilous pestilence" (Ps. 91:3).

"Don't go for the bread crumbs," Mike Brown warns in his book, *Avoiding the Snare (2007)*.

All that was required to construct the snare was a box, a long piece of twine, a short stick, and some bread crumbs. Do you remember engaging in snare activity? It was simple. Just prop the box up with the short stick. Bait the snare by placing a few bread crumbs under the propped box. Then tie the twine to the bottom of the stick and unroll the string to your hiding place in the bushes a few yards away and wait. Soon the birds came, enticed by the bread crumbs, venturing closer to the box and finally hopping underneath it to eat the small bits of bread. That's when you pulled the twine making the box fall trapping the bird inside!

It's a great illustration of what many of us have experienced in our lives. We have been enticed by what seemed desirable and maybe even thought to be necessary, only to find ourselves trapped and asking ourselves: How did this happen? How did I wind up in this situation?

Mike Brown states that the "supreme genius of a snare is that it's hidden, unrecognized, and seemingly harmless, trapping you before you even realize you are in danger" (2007). Have you been there? I know I have on more than one occasion.

The good news is God can deliver us from the snare and, better yet, enable us to avoid the "snares of life" altogether as we keep our eyes on Him and pursue His presence. So stop going after the bread crumbs and start running toward God!

--------⋊--------

Prayer Point
Lord, help me to recognize the bait of Satan and avoid its temptation. Help me to keep my eyes on You.

WONDERING MOMENTS/QUESTIONS TO PONDER
(Read Psalm 91:3.)

1. Describe a snare and its purpose.

_____

_____

_____

_____

_____

2. What is the genius of a snare?

_____

_____

_____

_____

_____

3. How can you avoid the snares in your life?

_____

_____

_____

_____

_____

41

REAL LEADERSHIP FLOWS FROM GENUINE RELATIONSHIPS

———◦∞◦———

"Let nothing be done through selfish ambition or conceit, but in lowliness of mind let each esteem others better than himself. Let each of you look out not only for his own interests, but also for the interests of others" (Phil. 2:3–4).

Several years ago, I was invited to join a group of pastors who were committed to becoming more effective leaders within the church and communities where they served. For twelve months, we met regularly. We read books about leadership; we listened to leaders who shared with us some fundamental principle concerning effective leadership; we shared dreams, visions, concerns with each other; and we prayed a lot!

The group was a significant part of my life, and I'm grateful to have had the experience. While the training was excellent, the real value was in the relationships formed with others who shared in my struggles and I in theirs. And to this day, I continue to be blessed by several who were a part of the journey that year.

It was during that year I came to realize effective leadership has more to do with genuine relationships than with particular methodologies.

It is quite funny, the things one remembers. Of the many books read and lessons taught that year, only three continue to influence my understanding of, and approach to leadership/relationships. All three principles are from the same source—a book written by Bob Farr entitled *Renovate Or Die*. First, only dead fish go with the flow all the time. Second, if you lead, you are going to bleed. And finally, don't let someone hold you hostage because He or she has a loud voice (2011). Well, that's it. Pretty silly, right?

I want to invite you to take just a few moments and reflect on the three principles with this thought in mind: What do these statements reveal about how I relate to others? You may be surprised! Or, maybe not.

Prayer Point
Lord, help me to remember that real leadership
is not about personal power; instead, it's about
authentic relationships. It's about serving others
in Your name.

WONDERING MOMENTS/QUESTIONS TO PONDER
(Read Philippians 2:3–4.)

———————◁———————

1. What does esteeming others better than yourself entail?

_____

_____

_____

_____

_____

2. How would you interpret Bob Farr's statement that "Only dead fish go with the flow all the time"?

_____

_____

_____

_____

_____

3. Do you agree or disagree with the statement that effective leadership has more to do with genuine relationships than with particular methodologies? Why or why not?

_____

_____

_____

_____

_____

42

MIRACLES HAPPEN

———————⟨∝⟩———————

"But Jesus looked at them and said, 'With men, it is impossible, but not with God; for with God all things are possible'" (Mark 10:27).

Miracles—we read about them in the Bible. We may even have prayed for a miracle. We might have heard someone speak of having been healed. But, do we—do I—believe that God is still performing miracles?

As a pastor, I have had the privilege of being invited into the lives of many during their moments of crises and asked to pray for God to perform a miracle; God, heal; God, deliver; God, restore; God, we need a miracle! And I have seen some who were quite ill get well. I have seen some who were bound by addiction delivered. I have seen some marriages that seemed broken beyond repair be restored. But I have also seen the sick die, the addicted remain in bondage, and marriages remain broken.

Why is it that, in some cases, the miraculous happens, and in others, it doesn't? Is it merely a matter of being lucky? Richard Dawkins seems to think so when he says, "Events that we commonly call miracles are not supernatural but are part of a spectrum of more or less improbable natural events. A miracle, in other words, if it occurs at all, is a tremendous stroke of luck." (Strobel, 2018).

On the other hand, John Lennox says, "God is not a prisoner of the laws of nature. God, who set the regularities there, can himself feed a new event into the system from outside. Science cannot stop Him from doing that." (Strobel, 2018). I like what C. S. Lewis says concerning the miraculous: "Miracles are a retelling in small letters of the very same story which is written across the whole world in letters to large for some of us to see." But I think I like what G. K. Chesterton says the best, and I believe it with all my heart, "The most incredible thing about miracles is that they happen!"(Strobel, 2018).

I don't know where or when; I just know God is still performing miracles! And today just might be such a day!

————————⟨∞⟩————————

Prayer Point
Lord, open the eyes of my heart so I might see the wondrous workings of Your might. I know Lord that all things are possible with You.

WONDERING MOMENTS/QUESTIONS TO PONDER
(Read Mark 10:27.)

———————⟨✕⟩———————

1. Do you believe God is still performing miracles?

_____

_____

_____

_____

_____

2. Have you ever prayed for a miracle, and it did not happen? How did it make you feel?

_____

_____

_____

_____

_____

3. Do you believe that all things are possible with God? Why or why not?

_____

_____

_____

_____

_____

43

START CLIMBING

———————⌧———————

"I can do all things through Christ who strengthens me" (Phil. 4:13).

Here's a bit of country wisdom from Kemmons Wilson to consider as you begin or end your day. "There are two ways to get to the top of an oak tree, find a healthy acorn, and sit on it and wait, or take hold of the first limb you can reach and start climbing."(Tanner, 1999).

How often have you and I been faced with a situation that seemed to be insurmountable? In those moments, what has been your response? There have been times when faced with a difficult situation, I have responded by giving up or giving in without making a determined effort to overcome it. I would think that I'm not alone in that response.

Life is hard at times. If we want to succeed, we must be determined to do so. John Wooden once said, "Do not let what you cannot do interfere with what you can do." (Tanner, 1999). And it was Albert Einstein who said, "In the middle of difficulty lies opportunity." (1999).

We have a choice in how we respond to the challenges we face. Paul tells us in Philippians 4:13, "I can do all things through Christ, which strengtheneth me." That's the key to climbing the tree of challenges we face in life. Do we trust God, or do we seek to live life in our strength?

Look, today, we can choose to sit and hope things resolve themselves. We can tell ourselves there's nothing we can do, or we can "take hold of the first limb, and in God's strength, begin to climb."

Be encouraged today when difficulties come your way, see the opportunities they present, and start climbing, not in your strength, but His!

———————✗———————

Prayer Point
Lord, I know that in You I can do all things
because there is nothing too difficult for You!

WONDERING MOMENTS/QUESTIONS TO PONDER
(Read Philippians 4:13.)

————————✕————————

1. Paul says we can do all things. How can we do all these things?

    _____

    _____

    _____

    _____

    _____

2. Have you ever known someone who would find a healthy acorn and sit on it, waiting for the oak to grow rather than take hold of the first limb and begin climbing?

    _____

    _____

    _____

    _____

    _____

3. From where does your strength come?

_____

_____

_____

_____

_____

44

THE ULTIMATE REALITY

———————⧓———————

"Fear not, for I am with you; Be not dismayed, for I am your God. I will strengthen you. Yes, I will help you; I will uphold you with My righteous right hand" (Isa. 4:10).

Has anyone ever said to you, or maybe you have said it to someone, "It's going to be okay—just hang on?" It's usually said to comfort and encourage another person in a moment of suffering or sadness. For the person who is suffering, believing all will be alright is not always easy. The question of *why?* often fills the mind of the one who is struggling. A question to which the answer can be elusive. We have all had moments when believing that everything is going to be okay is not what we are feeling.

I love this quote by John Lennon, "Everything will be all right in the end. If it's not all right, it's not yet the end." (Rohr, 2019). The statement reflects the belief that everything in the universe is moving toward an ultimate reality, and that reality is the goodness of God, who created all things and called them good! It is God who is determined to restore all things, and that includes you and me and the other!

So, keep moving even when things are not all right. Remember, God, who is Good, is bringing everything in line with the "ultimate reality" of His goodness and love. Listen, if everything is not all right yet, hang on; it soon will be!

Prayer Point

Lord, grant me the tenacity to hang on to You amid the difficulties of life. Help me to remember in those moments that You are restoring all things unto Yourself, and You are good. Life, when lived in Your presence, is good!

WONDERING MOMENTS/A QUESTION TO PONDER
(Read Isaiah 4:10.)

———————◇———————

Spend some time reflecting on the question, "What if everything isn't going to be okay? Are you alright with that?

45

HOW IS YOUR DASH?

———————————⚬———————————

*"As you, therefore, have received Christ Jesus the Lord,
so walk in Him, rooted and built up in Him and
established in the faith, as you have been taught,
abounding in it with thanksgiving" (Col 2:6–7).*

Linda Ellis tells us that, "Our lives consist of two dates and a dash, and it is the dash that really matters!"(Tanner, 1999). The first date is the date of your birth, and the second is the date of your death. A dash separates the two periods. The dash represents everything you've done during your lifetime.

How is your dash? We all want our lives to matter. I attended a meeting some years ago on leadership, and the speaker quoted from the poem by Ellis, "The Dash," (1996) and then asked the question, "Are you living your dash well?" He then went on to say, "If you want to have a decisive influence in the lives of those around you, sit at the feet of Christ each day, and then tell the world what you have seen."

The speaker went on to state, "The measure of our influence is directly related to our intimacy with Christ." It is in yielding to Christ that we influence others in positive ways.

We must make spending time with Christ a priority. If you and I want our "dash" to have meaning, spending quality time with Jesus is the key!

———————⟨×⟩———————

Prayer Point

Lord, may I not waste one moment but live every moment in obedience to Your will. Lord, may You not be one of many priorities but **the priority** *of my life.*

WONDERING MOMENTS/A QUESTION TO PONDER
(Read Colossians 2:6–7.)

———————✕———————

There are two dates, Linda Ellis, tells us and in between them is a dash. That dash, she says, represents everything you've done during your lifetime. Spend a few moments responding to the question, "How is your dash going?

46

WHO'S YOUR FREDDIE?

———————◇———————

"A disciple is not above his teacher, but everyone who is perfectly trained will be like his teacher" (Luke 6:40).

Tripp Bowden, in his book, *Freddie and Me,* shares many of the life lessons he learned from Freddie Bennett, the legendary caddy master at Augusta National. In the book, Bowden tells the story of his life-transforming friendship with the famed caddy master. He concludes the book by asking, "Who is the Freddie in your life?" (2009). We all need a Freddie in our lives. Someone who will tell it like it is. Someone who will both challenge and encourage us, someone who will go beyond the expected; and we need someone who will believe in us when we fail to believe in ourselves.

One of the Freddie-isms Bowden grew to love was, "Don't ever tell anybody to lay up on the chance of a lifetime." Another was, "Even the best golfer in the world isn't as perfect as he might appear. You ain't gotta be perfect to succeed!" (2009).

While it is true we all need a "Freddie" in our lives, it is also true that as Christians, we are called to be a "Freddie" in someone else's life. And remember, "You ain't gotta be perfect; you just need to be you"!

———————⚭———————

Prayer Point
Lord, as I go about today, keep me aware that my actions influence others. I pray that in all I do and say, You would be exalted!

WONDERING MOMENTS/A QUESTION TO PONDER
(Read Luke 6:40.)

————————⊂⊃————————

"You ain't gotta be perfect; you just need to be you." What does that mean for you? Write about it.

47

SEE HIS GRACE

———————◇———————

"But as you abound in everything—in faith, in speech, in knowledge, in all diligence, and in your love for us— see that you abound in this grace also" (2 Cor. 8:7).

"Alongside them, we felt like grasshoppers. And they looked down on us as if we were grasshoppers" (Num. 13:33).

He was a church-going Bible-believing God-fearing man. He had never married, not that he didn't want to; he just never did. He now found himself in a hospital, gasping for breath, alone, rejected, and dying. Alone and rejected because of the rumors. You see, some years earlier, he had been in a severe car accident and, during surgery, had received several pints of blood. The blood was infected with HIV. And now, he was dying. The rumor was that he was gay. You can understand, can't you? He was fifty years old and had never been married and was now dying with AIDs. The thing that hurt most was he had always loved the church and God's people. But now where were they? He hadn't seen anyone for several months, and he knew the rumors.

Beside his bed there lay a Bible; as the nurse entered the room she saw it, sat down, and began to read from Psalm 23. "The Lord is my Shepherd ..." His struggled breathing seemed to calm somewhat as she read. Suddenly the nurse stopped reading as she felt his touch upon her hand; as she looked, he smiled and died.

What is it that empowers individuals like Joshua and Caleb and this man dying with AIDs, rejected by those he loved? The word for me, and I believe it to be from the Lord, is *wonder*: the Wonder and majesty of God's grace. They knew and had experienced the wonderful grace of God!

———————✕———————

Prayer Point
Lord, give me eyes to see the wonder and splendor of Your grace and the courage to share that grace with others.

WONDERING MOMENTS/A QUESTION TO PONDER
(Read 2 Corinthians 8:7.)

———————◇———————

God's grace is all around us. Think about a time when God's grace was especially evident to you and write as you remember.

48

TIME MATTERS

―――――――――∝―――――――――

"See then that you walk circumspectly, not as fools but as wise, redeeming the time, because the days are evil" *(Eph. 5:15–16).*

Have you heard the phrase, "Time is of the essence?" It is a phrase used to communicate the importance of a task being completed. Time and how we spend it matters. I remember being told on several occasions, "Sam, stop wasting time—get to work!" As much I hated hearing it, time is of the essence. Time does matter!

John Elliot states, "There are ten things that we must always take time to do, even if we feel as though we haven't the time to do them."(Tanner, 1999). Here they are:

Take time to work—it is the price of success.
Take time to think—it is the source of power.
Take time to play—it is the secret of youth.
Take time to read—it is the foundation of knowledge.
Take time to worship—it is the highway of reverence and washes the dust of the Earth from our eyes.
Take time to help and enjoy friends—it is the source of happiness.

Take time to love—it is the sacrament of life.
Take time to dream—it hitches the soul to the stars.
Take time to laugh—it is the singing that helps with life's loads, and:
Take time to plan—it is the secret of being able to have time to make time for the first nine things.

———————⋈———————

Prayer Point
***Lord, may I not waste time today but take time to
do the things that matter to You.***

WONDERING MOMENTS/QUESTIONS TO PONDER
(Read Ephesians 5:15–16.)

———————⟨✕⟩———————

1. Why do you think that time is of the essence?

———————————————————————————

———————————————————————————

———————————————————————————

———————————————————————————

———————————————————————————

2. What steps can you take not to waste time?

———————————————————————————

———————————————————————————

———————————————————————————

———————————————————————————

———————————————————————————

49

UNCONDITIONAL

———————————∽———————————

"Behold what manner of love the Father has bestowed on us, that we should be called children of God! Therefore the world does not know us because it did not know Him" (1 John 3:1).

She loved her dad very much, and she knew that he loved her. But what was she to do now? What would he say when he found out? She had made some bad decisions in her life, and he had always stood with her no matter the issue. But now, what about now? She was a college student, unmarried, and pregnant. Her greatest fear was that this would be the final straw, and he would say enough is enough and wash his hands of her. She wouldn't blame him if he did. The good news is that he didn't; he still loved his daughter very much.

Without going into a lot of detail, I was a young pastor, and she came into my office and shared her situation with me. After a great deal of listening and praying together, she agreed to allow me to set up a meeting with her and her dad and me as a third, "objective" person.

I witness something unexpected. I saw a dad listen to a wayward daughter. There was no scolding, no anger—just a broken heart for his struggling and fearful daughter. He assured her that both her mother and he would stand with her. He was disappointed to be sure, but his love for his daughter was unconditional. Nothing would ever change that! I don't know who was crying more, me or them. It was an incredible moment for them to be sure, but also for me. I saw at that moment a portrait of God's unconditional love.

She went on to have the child, and with the help of her parents, she finished college, Today she is happily married and has two children she adores and loves unconditionally. God's love is unwavering. He never gives up on us. We are loved, and that's a fact!

---------------◯✕◯---------------

Prayer Point
Lord, Your love for me is beyond measure. Your love is a love not rooted in performance. It is who You are. Fill me, Lord, with Your love so I too may love as You love.

WONDERING MOMENTS/QUESTIONS TO PONDER
(Read 1 John 3:1.)

————————◇————————

1. What does it mean to be a child of God?

_____

_____

_____

_____

_____

2. How was the young college student's dad like our heavenly Father?

_____

_____

_____

_____

3. What does unconditional love mean to you?

_____

_____

50

SWIMMING UPSTREAM

———————— ✕ ————————

"Therefore, since Christ suffered for us in the flesh, arm yourselves also with the same mind, for he who has suffered in the flesh has ceased from sin, that he no longer should live the rest of his time in the flesh for the lusts of men, but for the will of God" (1 Peter 4:1–2).

Are you confident you're doing what God created you to do? It's a good question. It's one Andrew Wommack asks in his book entitled *How to Find, Follow, and Fulfill God's Will*. He says that he is no longer surprised by the number of Christians who are uncertain of their purpose. Many are doing good things but feel unfulfilled (2013). I have felt that way at times. How about you? Are you sure you're in God's will for your life?

You and I aren't going to fulfill God's will accidentally. We don't just stumble into it. We must be intentional in our pursuit of God's will! According to Wommack, it's human nature to seek the path of least resistance. As a result, many go through life, allowing obstacles they encounter to determine what direction they take (2013).

It doesn't have to be like that. God longs for us to experience the contentment of a well-lived life. To experience that life, we must do more than just go with the flow. Wommack put it this way: even a dead fish can float downstream (2013).

Doing God's will often calls us to swim upstream against the flow of today's cultural norms. It's not easy, and we are unable to do so without the power of the Holy Spirit. It is God's Spirit that creates in us a deep desire to fulfill our purpose for being. Knowing you are in God's will brings a sense of peace, even when swimming upstream!

Prayer Point

Lord, grant me the courage to swim upstream when necessary, knowing that You who designed me will also empower me!

WONDERING MOMENTS/A
QUESTION TO PONDER
(Read 1 Peter 4:1–2.)

———————∝———————

As Christians in today's secular culture, we often find ourselves at odds with socially acceptable norms. We often find ourselves moving in the opposite direction. Have you experienced this "swimming upstream" against the "cultural current"? As Christians, how are we to remain faithful to God's will when everyone else seems to be going the other way?

51

RECEPTIVE

———⟨✕⟩———

"I beseech you therefore, brethren, by the mercies of God, that you present your bodies a living sacrifice, holy, acceptable to God, which is your reasonable service. And do not be conformed to this world, but be transformed by the renewing of your mind, that you may prove what is that good and acceptable and perfect will of God" (Rom. 12:1–2).

How do we do it? In a culture that values independence and self-reliance, how do we yield to what God is doing? Living a yielded life doesn't just happen. Embracing what God desires to do for us is not easy. It requires a new way of thinking on our part. It requires a transformation, a renewing of our mind. Receiving what God has for us and wants to do in us requires preparation of the soul. Much like the farmer prepares the soil to receive the seed and germinate, so we must prepare our souls to receive God's blessings.

Living a blessed life isn't happenstance. It happens because your heart has been made receptive to His will. It's like lightning. Many think that lightning comes down from the sky. It looks that way, but there is a negative charge in the ground that attracts lightning. You can see this in time-lapse photos of a lightning strike. So lightning actually starts in the ground. The reality is that it strikes certain places for a reason—the ground is receptive, and as a result, draws the lightning to it. In the same way, it is the heart that has been cultivated to receive the blessings of God that attract those blessings.

Are you experiencing the blessings of God? If not, it might be wise to prepare the ground of your heart to be more receptive to His presence and thereby more open to His blessings.

―――――――――――⋈―――――――――――

Prayer Point
Lord, may I diligently study Your Word, preparing my heart to be more receptive to your blessings.

WONDERING MOMENTS/A QUESTION TO PONDER
(Read Romans 12:1–2.)

———————◇———————

Living a blessed life doesn't just happen. It happens because you have made your heart receptive to God's will. What are some things you can do to make your heart more receptive to God's will?

52

JACK DANIELS OR JESUS?

———————◇———————

"Jesus answered him, 'The first of all, the commandments is "Hear, O Israel, the Lord our God, the Lord is one. And you shall love the Lord your God with all your heart, with all your soul, with all your mind, and with all your strength. This is the first commandment."' And the second, like it, is this: 'You shall love your neighbor as yourself.' There is no other commandment greater than these." (Mark 12:28–31)

It was Sunday morning, and he had decided that this would be the Sunday he would give the church a try. His life had become one of brokenness and disappointment. His marriage had failed, his job was in jeopardy, and his best friend was a pint of Jack Daniels. He was searching. He knew there had to be more to life than what he was experiencing.

As he entered the sanctuary of the church, the choir was singing the song—"Holy Ground." On the walls hung banners. One banner caught his eye—it read GOD IS LOVE. He took a deep breath and thought maybe this was the answer to his troubled life. He had grown up in the church but had not been since he first went to college, and that was over twenty years ago. He was desperate and searching.

Following the service, the people spoke to one another. They hugged each other. No one talked to or hugged him. He left, having come hoping to find something that would give him a reason to go on, unconvinced that God or anyone loved him!

Every day, some cross our path who need to know that they are loved. They need to know they matter to somebody. Do we see them? Do we hear their cry, and do we respond as those who know the love of God? As Christians, we are called to love God with all our being and to love others. That's it! So, how are you doing? Do you love others? Are others encountering the reality of God's love for them because of you and me, or are they crossing our paths without experiencing God's love?

Today, may our eyes be open to seeing, our ears open to hearing, and our hearts open to embrace those around us, who are desperate to know that they are loved! Remember, as Christian, you and I have only two things by which our life is to be defined: loving God and loving people.

------------×------------

Prayer Point
Lord, open my eyes so I might see those who are desperate to know Your love tangibly. Use me, Lord, as an instrument of Your love.

WONDERING MOMENTS/QUESTIONS TO PONDER
(Read Mark 12:28–31.)

———————⟨✕⟩———————

1. It's sad to say, but some churches are more concerned with their image than they are with broken and hurting people. What does it mean to love God with all your heart, soul, mind, and strength?

_____

_____

_____

_____

_____

2. What does it mean to love your neighbor as yourself?

_____

_____

_____

_____

_____

53

REFRESHING RAIN

———————◇———————

*"Behold therefore and be converted that your sins may
be blotted out, so that times of refreshing may come
from the presence of the Lord" (Acts 3:12).*

Have you ever experienced a sense of total exhaustion or felt
hopeless or overwhelmed? If you have, know that you aren't
alone in feeling that way. We all face hardships and difficulties in
our lives. I think it is a part of living in a fallen world. In those
moments, the last thing you want to hear is, "Man up," or, "Get over
it already." That's what was said to me by a district superintendent
some years ago.

I had come to him, seeking encouragement and insight. I was
struggling as a pastor. I was also experiencing major depression. All
I knew was that I was hurting, and I felt a sense of guilt because, as
a pastor, I shouldn't have such moments—Right? I heard once that
"only one in forty pastors will make it to retirement." I was about to
become one of those thirty-nine. I was tired, burned out, and to tell
you the truth; I didn't like being around people. I was desperate and
in trouble—emotionally speaking. I left discouraged and ashamed
that I felt that way, and I was angry!

Something had to change! I needed a fresh wind to blow over me. I needed a renewed sense of God's call upon my life. I remember reaching over to the seat next to me in my car, picking up my Bible, and praying, "God, I'm tired, and unless you renew my spirit, I'm done!" As I prayed the thought, *Turn to Acts 3:19* came into my mind. So, I turned to the text and read, "Now it's time to change your way! Turn to face God so He can wipe away your sins, pour out showers of blessings, and refresh you as you come into His presence." I began to weep as I sensed His presence. It was for me an Upper Room experience—it just happened to be in my car. I can't tell you that my struggles instantly disappeared, but I did begin to feel God's presence with me. I began to preach and teach and pray and serve with a deeper awareness of God's presence with me and His love for me.

Experiencing the refreshing rain of God's presence is found in turning away from our agendas and turning toward and fulfilling His.

————————⟨✕⟩————————

Prayer Point
Lord, may I turn to You and Your plan and, by doing so, experience the refreshing rain of Your presence.

WONDERING MOMENTS/QUESTIONS TO PONDER
(Read Acts 3:12.)

————————⟨✕⟩————————

1. Think about a time when you've been completely exhausted. How did you feel physically, emotionally, and spiritually? Reflect briefly on those feelings.

    _____

    _____

    _____

    _____

    _____

2. Now think of a time when you experienced a sense of renewal—a time of being refreshed. Reflect briefly on that experience.

    _____

    _____

    _____

    _____

    _____

54

LOVE LETTERS

———◇———

"And we have known and believed the love that God has for us. God is love, and he who abides in love abides in God and God in him" (1 John 4:16).

"Roses are red, and Violets are blue, girl you look good, and I like you! Will you be my girlfriend? Check Yes or No." There, you have it, the first love note I ever wrote. I know; it's not Robert Frost but not bad for a third grader.

It was the first love note I ever wrote. I was in love with the girl who sat in front of Jimmy, who sat in front of me. The day came when I found the courage to let her know how I felt. My only problem was Jimmy. How was I to get the note to her without Jimmy reading it first? I had no choice but to give the letter to Jimmy. So, I gave the message to Jimmy, and he passed it forward to her. I watched as she unfolded the note and began to read. I could hardly breathe. She soon returned the letter. Her reply wasn't what I had hoped. She had responded by writing, "Sammy, you're okay, but so is Jimmy; it all depends on what you will give me."

How often have we experienced conditional love? I will love you if you do this or act like this or give me what I want? The good news is that God doesn't love that way. His love is unconditional and inclusive. His love for us is not based on performance. His passion is always present. It's all around us, but there are so many who fail to see it.

I'm convinced that as Christians, we are a love letter from God to a broken and hurting world. We are to live in such a way that others will see and experience His love through us. And, as a result, say, "Yes" to a relationship with Him.

———————⌑———————

Prayer Point
Lord, may I be a love letter from You to those who
have yet to see and experience Your great love.

WONDERING MOMENTS/QUESTIONS TO PONDER
(Read 1 John 4:16.)

———————⋈———————

1. Have you ever written a love letter or received a love letter? How did it make you feel?

_____

_____

_____

_____

_____

2. Have you experienced conditional love? How did you feel?

_____

_____

_____

_____

_____

3. What is the difference between love based on conditions and love that is unconditional?

_____

_____

_____

_____

_____

55

GOD'S KINGDOM CHOIR

———————∝———————

"May our dependably steady and warmly personal God develop maturity in you so that you get along with each other, as well as Jesus, get along with us all. Then we'll be a choir—not our voices only, but our very lives, singing in harmony in a stunning anthem to the God and Father of our Master Jesus" (Rom. 15:5–6, The Message).

There is nothing more moving or powerful than a grand choir, where each section sings its part with precision, passion, and anointing. One of the greatest choral groups I have ever heard was the Junaluska Singers, directed by Dr. Glenn Draper.

I remember sitting in the congregation as the choir formed a circle around us and with perfect pitch and in perfect harmony, without music, sang "Amazing Grace." It was an unforgettable moment.

I believe that God would have the church to be like that, to encircle the world and sing in perfect harmony the message of His amazing grace. There are four things I believe God longs to see and to hear in the church and our personal lives, that when done in faith, sounds forth an anthem that can change the world.

First, He longs for our faith to be authentic. Next, He desires that we have a servant's heart. Third, He wants us to be a people of the Word, not only hearing the Word but living it as well. Finally, God longs for the church to welcome all people, not just some!

When we, the church, live according to these principles, our lives become a part of that kingdom choir, singing in perfect harmony the wonders of His grace. How awesome is that?

Prayer Point
Lord, may I endeavor to sing my part in Your kingdom choir, and may the world both see and hear the message of Your marvelous grace.

WONDERING MOMENTS/A QUESTION TO PONDER
(Read Romans 15:5–6.)

———————◇———————

Paul speaks of living harmoniously with one another, like a choir singing in harmony. Share your thoughts about living in harmony with each other. In a choir, sections are singing specific parts, and when put together, it results in a stunning anthem. How does that image relate to how we are to live with one another?

56

A CRACKER AND A CUP OF APPLE JUICE

───────◇───────

"Let us, therefore, come boldly to the throne of grace, that we may obtain mercy and find grace to help in time of need" (Heb. 4:16).

I hadn't heard from her in years. There was a time when she called almost weekly just to talk. We had never dated, but we were close and could share just about anything with each other. I remember our conversations always ended with me, saying, "Remember, you are loved." And she would always respond with, "Yeah, I know God loves me." I was surprised when I answered the phone and heard her voice. It had been so long since we had talked, and she sounded timid and frightened. She wasted no time. "Sam, can you come and see me? I'm very sick, and I just need to see you," I told her I would come. So, the following day I drove three hours to the hospital. When I arrived, I was shocked by what I saw. A once beautiful and vibrant person was now thin and very sick.

As I entered her room, she reached out to take my hand and held it as she talked about her life—a life of brokenness. She had turned to alcohol and drugs. She was ashamed, afraid, and alone.

She began to cry as we talked. I remember being uncomfortable, not knowing what to say. I remember praying silently, "God, what am I to do?" I looked around the room and saw some crackers and some juice sitting on her tray table. I reached over, took the crackers and juice, and asked would she mind if we shared communion. At first, she refused, saying she wasn't worthy to receive. She began to cry, and so did I, as the presence of the Lord filled the room. I handed a cracker to her and said, "This is His body given for you." I then gave her the cup of juice and said, "This is His blood shed for you." As she ate the cracker and drank the juice, she began to weep, saying over and over—He does, He does love me! Yes, He does, and so do I.

At that moment, she seemed more beautiful, even in her sickness and impending death. We continued to talk for hours, crying and laughing together. It would be the last time we shared, but before I left, she asked, "How do I tell Him that I love Him and ask Him to forgive me?' I said, "Just tell Him. He knows your heart." She did tell Him she loved Him, and as I was leaving, I turned and said what I always said, "Remember, you are loved. Always! Nothing can ever change that."

It was to be our last conversation; she died three days later. But she was alive in those three days more than she had ever been. It was just a cracker and a cup of apple juice. No, it was much more than that! It was God's divine embrace, and it changed her life and mine.

———————⌖———————

Prayer Point
Lord, help me to remember I am loved, always, no matter what!

WONDERING MOMENTS/A QUESTION TO PONDER
(Read Hebrews 4:16.)

———————◦×◦———————

The writer of Hebrews instructs us to come boldly to the throne of grace. Here the word *boldly* means a frankness of speech, so bold it often met with resistance. How is it that we can come boldly to the throne of grace?

57

BUSY GOING NOWHERE

———⚬———

"For My flesh is food indeed, and My blood is drink indeed. He who eats My flesh and drinks My blood abides in Me, and I in him. As the living Father sent Me, and I live because of the Father, so he who feeds on Me will live because of Me. This is the bread which came down from heaven—not as your fathers ate the manna and are dead. He who eats this bread will live forever" (John 6:55–58).

I saw it on a church sign while driving. "You're so busy going nowhere; It won't be long before you get there." It's like going on a Sunday afternoon drive. We aren't headed anywhere in particular; we're just driving around and looking out the window. Living life without a purpose isn't living at all.

Still, many people live their lives that way. Maybe you're one of them. Your life's story has no plot, and a story without a plot is no real story at all. It's like the man who said to the doctor when told he was dying, "What do you mean, I'm dying! I'm not sure I've ever gotten around to living."

Some are exerting so much energy trying to be someone whom they are not. I don't want to be that person, and I don't think you do either. We shouldn't play the "Game of Life" wearing someone else's jersey when we've been given one of our own. There is for each of us a divine purpose for being. God created you and me for a reason. We will never know true contentment or fulfillment until we are living out that purpose. I don't want to live what one man described as "a decaffeinated life."

How about you? It's time to wake up and not just smell the coffee, but drink it! Claim the life that God has for you, and don't look back. God created each of us for a divine purpose. I don't want to settle for anything less than God's best, nor should you!

------------◇------------

Prayer Point
Lord, let me not settle for less than You have for me. You are my Creator, and You know what is best for me. Lord, today I commit myself to pursue all that You have planned for my life.

WONDERING MOMENTS/A QUESTION TO PONDER
(Read John 6:55–58.)

———————◇———————

What do you think is meant by Jesus when He said, "Whoever feeds on Me will live"?

_____

_____

_____

_____

_____

58

GET AFTER IT!

———————⋈———————

"Give no sleep to your eyes nor slumber to your eyelids"
(Prov. 6:4).

*F*riends *Like You* is an album by singer and songwriter Al Holley. My favorite song on the album is entitled "Come Next Spring." It's a song with a powerful message. It speaks of our tendency to put off the thing we need to do today until tomorrow, but the sad truth is that for many, tomorrows never come (1980).

She had been molested as a child by an uncle. She never told her parents or anyone for that matter. In high school, she began attending parties and drinking heavily. Her drinking was out of control. Her parents demanded that she see a counselor. The counselor told her on several occasions that she needed to stop the drinking. Her response was always the same; I know, and I will. One night after attending a party and having had way too much to drink, while on her way home, she ran off the road and hit a tree. She died later that evening from the injuries she sustained. She had promised them she would stop drinking. And she was going to—tomorrow, but tomorrow never came.

I remember a message I once heard on an answering machine. "Sorry, we can't take your call at the moment because we are out taking advantage of the little opportunities that are making themselves available; hope you're doing the same. Leave your name and number, and we'll call you back." I love that message!

Every day there are things we need to do—some opportunities we need to act on, something that must be done. We have today, and tomorrow may not come, so wake up and *get after it*!

———————⋈———————

Prayer Point
Lord, may I not waste time today. May I do the things that You have called me to do today!

WONDERING MOMENTS/A QUESTION TO PONDER
(Read Proverbs 6:4.)

———————✠———————

Why do you think people often put off things that need to be done now until later?

_____

_____

_____

_____

_____

59

PICK UP YOUR BANJO AND START SINGING

---✕---

"I will bless the Lord at all times; His praise shall continually be in my mouth. My soul shall make its boast in the Lord; The humble shall hear of it and be glad. Oh, magnify the Lord with me, and let us exalt His name together" (Ps. 34:1–3).

I was looking for something the other day, and during my search I looked in a box, thinking it might be there, but it wasn't. There was, however, a small book that had been given to me by my sister Kay. I'm sure many of you have read the book by Diane Muldrow, *Everything I Need to Know I Learned From a Little Golden Book*. I picked up the book and, forgetting what it was I was looking for, began to read.

As I read, one page caught my attention. It was beautifully illustrated. There was a young child dressed as a cowboy and sitting in a field on a stump, playing the banjo and singing. The sentence at the top of the page read, "Sing even if you can't hold a tune" (Muldrow, 2013).

I've been unable to get that picture and caption out of my mind. For the past several weeks, when faced with both physical and emotional challenges, the image floods my mind, and I smile and sing, and press on. It's a small thing I know and a bit silly, but it has been an empowering and freeing image for me. I'm often frustrated because of the challenges that come when living with Parkinson's disease. There are days when getting out of bed is difficult, and days when I'm easily agitated and don't respond to stress very well. There are days when I can't remember things that I should know, and there are times when my thinking process is tremendously slowed. It's on days like these that I need to "sing even if I can't hold a tune."

Parkinson's disease has had a significant impact on my life, but it doesn't have to define it. I can't do things like I once could, and that can be very frustrating. But, it's up to me whether I allow it to rob me of joy or not.

All of us have challenges in life. And, we all have a decision to make. Do we allow the difficulties that may come our way to take our joy and our will to overcome, or do we pick up the banjo and start singing—even if we can't hold a tune? The choice is ours to make. I want to sing even though I may be a bit off-key. How about you? *Just pick up the banjo and start singing*!

———————✕———————

Prayer Point

Lord, today may I have the courage to sing, rather than sit around pouting. May I press on, rather than give up, and may I serve You, rather than my self-interests. And as I do so, may others hear the sweet melody of Your grace being sung through my life to those who are themselves facing tremendous challenges.

WONDERING MOMENTS/QUESTIONS TO PONDER
(Read Psalm 34:1–3.)

———————◇———————

1. What does it mean to bless the Lord at all times?

   _____

   _____

   _____

   _____

   _____

2. What does the phrase "Sing even if you can't hold a tune" mean to you?

   _____

   _____

   _____

   _____

   _____

60

MY DAD, A
COTTONMOUTH, AND ME

———◇———

"For when we were still without strength, in due time,
Christ died for the ungodly. For scarcely for a righteous
man will one die, yet perhaps for a good man, someone
would even dare to die. But God demonstrates His
own love toward us, in that while we were still sinners,
Christ died for us" (Rom. 5:6–8).

The trip was unforgettable. My dad and I floated almost a hundred miles down the Flint River from Thomaston, Georgia, to Lake Blackshear in Warwick, Georgia. It remains one of the greatest memories of my life.

It wasn't an easy trip without challenges. The river was low, and there were several spots along the way, where it became necessary to carry the boat a short distance before putting it back into the river and continuing the trip. Each night we made camp on a sandbar. The scenery along the river was beautiful. We talked and fished and just spent time together, just my dad and me. It's a trip I'll always treasure.

I remember it raining at one point along the way, and everything was soaked, especially us. As we approached a bridge near the city of Montezuma, dad suggested we secure the boat under the bridge and find a motel so we could dry out. That's when it happened, the moment I'll never forget. As we climbed up the hill to the road above and began our walk into town, dad suddenly pushed me back, and stepped in front of me. Stretching out his arms, he yelled, "Stop!" In front of us was a large cottonmouth moccasin. The cottonmouth is an aggressive, venomous snake that is semi-aquatic. Dad was putting himself at risk to protect me! We carefully made our way around the snake and continued into town. The next morning we returned to the river and continued our trip, arriving safely at our pick-up point.

I've told the story many times over the years in sermons I've preached. What my dad did in pushing me back and stepping in front of me, is for me a vivid picture of what our heavenly Father has done through Jesus Christ at Calvary's Cross. Sin is an aggressive and venomous snake that will do great harm if permitted.

The good news, however, is that Christ has stepped in front, stretched out his arms, and has shouted, "Stop!" I'll never forget that trip and what Dad did to protect me from harm. More importantly, I'll always remember what my Father has done for me through Christ!

———————◇———————

Prayer Point
Lord, I thank You for leading me and guiding me.
Thank you for protecting me from the deadly strike
of sin. Help me to trust You in all things.

WONDERING MOMENTS/A QUESTION TO PONDER
(Read Romans 5 6–8.)

———◇———

In what ways does the story of my dad's actions, when confronting the danger of a cottonmouth, illustrate what Christ has done for us at Calvary?

61

THE POWER OF A HUG

———◇———

"Beloved, let us love one another, for love is of God,
and everyone who loves is born of God and knows
God. 1John 4: 8

I t was a crisp, Thursday afternoon in Dallas, Texas, in the fall of
1983. A group of us from Criswell Bible College gathered on
the steps of the federal courthouse in downtown Dallas. We were
doing what we did every Thursday afternoon, sharing our faith with
anyone who would listen. Most of the people just rolled their eyes
and kept on walking, and we would keep on preaching. But, this
would be a different Thursday. This Thursday, my life would be profoundly changed.

As the team was sharing with several people, all of whom looked
to be well off. I noticed a woman digging through a trash can in
search of food. Her clothes were filthy, and she smelled. I remember
thinking, *Why is no one sharing with this poor woman?* I turned to
our evangelism professor, Dr. Allen Street, and in a tone of self-righ-
teousness, voiced my concern. His reply wasn't what I expected;
"Mr. Wilder," he said, "I see that you are available." His rebuke awak-
ened me to the reality of my prejudice. He continued by saying, "I

suggest that you go and share with her!" *Me and my big mouth*, I thought. I reluctantly walked over to her, almost sickened by the smell. I tapped her on the shoulder, and she turned to face me. I told her who I was and that God loved her. She responded as she returned to digging through the trash can, "Don't bother; I've heard it all before."

Before I realized what I was doing, I asked if I could hug her? She looked at me for a moment and said, "If you would like." So I did, and as I hugged her—I promise you, I could no longer smell the offensive odor. We hugged for a few moments, and then, I stepped back and looked at her. I saw tears streaming down her face. She told me that it had been years since anyone had hugged her. I said to her, "God really does love you," and she said, "Maybe so." I told her He does. God loves you very much.

I learned that day that God's love must be enfleshed by those who know Him. It's not enough to speak it. We must embody it, even when it is difficult. Remember, it is the Holy Spirit that empowers us to love! *So stop holding back, and start loving*!

———————⋈———————

Prayer Point
Lord, may I not just talk about Your love, but empower me to share your love with everyone around me.

WONDERING MOMENTS/QUESTIONS TO PONDER
(Read 1 John 4:8.)

———————◇———————

1. Have you been guilty of avoiding certain people because they made you uncomfortable or because they were different?

_____

_____

_____

_____

_____

2. What do you think it means to enflesh God's love?

_____

_____

_____

_____

_____

62

STOP SPINNING AND START LIVING

———◇———

"Barricade the road that goes Nowhere; grace me with your clear revelation. I choose the true road to Somewhere; I post your road signs at every curve and corner" (Psalm 119:29–30, The Message)

For Christmas one year, I bought a Recumbent Exercise Bike. It's an incredible machine. I ride it every morning. It's equipped with a seven-inch smart HD touchscreen on which I can stream video workouts with world-class trainers from different locations around the globe. The areas from which these trainers produce their videos are some of the most beautiful places on the planet. I enjoy the workouts and the different places I get to view.

However, the truth remains that no matter how hard I pedal, at the end of the workout, I'm still in the same spot. I've seen the images, but I haven't been there.

It's a good illustration, depicting the reality of many. People pedal hard and never arrive at the place they want to be. Wow! How depressing—sorry! The point is that it doesn't have to be our experience. We don't have to spend our lives spinning our wheels. We can live a life of purpose and meaning. We can experience the splendor of life when living in God's grace, aware of His great love for us!

So, let's stop spinning our wheels going nowhere fast, and dreaming of what could have been. And let's start living a life of purpose that comes when we live for Him. It's when we yield to Christ that we truly experience the wonder and beauty of life.

------------------⋈------------------

Prayer Point
Lord, guide me as I seek to live a purposeful life. Keep me from the road to Nowhere, and by Your grace, may I choose the right path that leads to the destiny You have planned for me.

WONDERING MOMENTS/QUESTIONS TO PONDER
(Read Psalm 119:29–30.)

———————◇———————

1. Has there ever been a period in your life when you felt as though you were working hard but were getting nowhere?

_____

_____

_____

_____

2. How do you move from just spinning your wheels to going somewhere?

_____

_____

_____

_____

_____

63

STOP WHINING

———∞———

"Now you are the body of Christ, and members individually" (1 Cor. 12:27).

The caption read, "We will never change the world by going to church. We will only change the world by *being* the church." Having been a pastor for over thirty years, I've come to recognize the tremendous value of attending church. To gather with others, to be a part of a community of faith is a source of strength and encouragement. But, just because a person attends church regularly doesn't mean that he or she is a true believer. Many in the church are religious. They play the part of having faith yet lack faith. I once heard it said that we gather to be renewed and empowered, and then "scatter to matter!"

I heard a song sung by Amy Grant called "Fat Babies." In the song, there is a powerful message. The song talks of sitting at the table of the sacred and feasting on the goodness of God's grace but never exercising faith. They grow "spiritually fat." They know of God but don't have a relationship with God. Their demand is always—feed me! Their complaint is still—I'm not being fed enough!

The apostle Paul, in 1Corinthians 12: 27, speaks of the church as being the "body of Christ." What does it mean to be a part of His body? It certainly means more than sitting around with a group of individuals who are just like you. You and I, as a part of His body, the church, are to be the visible and tangible expression of Christ's presence in the world as we live our lives being an instrument of God's transforming love.

————————◇————————

Prayer Point
Lord, may I not be guilty of whining like a fat baby, and make me a productive member of Your body, the church.

WONDERING MOMENTS/A
QUESTION TO PONDER
(Read 1 Corinthians 12:27.)

———————$\propto$———————

There are a lot of parts to the body, each serving a specific purpose. As with the human body, the body of Christ, the church, has many members. What does it mean to be a faithful member of Christ's body?

64

WHO'S GOING TO HOLD MY HAND

———⟨×⟩———

"Do not withhold good from those to whom it is due when it is in the power of your hand to do so" (Prov. 3:27).

They had been married for over sixty years when I first met them. They were amazing, funny, full of life, and very much in love. I had once asked them what the secret to their marriage was. He looked at me and said, "She needed me, and besides that, she can cook really well!" He went on to tell me that she wasn't half bad at keeping the yard and the house clean. As he spoke, I couldn't help but notice that she never let go of his hand, and she never stopped gazing at him and smiling.

Their love for each other was genuine. I remember she punched him in the arm when he said, "It just made sense to keep her around— you don't come across a gal like her very often; Oh, and she kisses really well!" I enjoyed visiting this couple. I loved listening to the story of their life together.

I remember the day of his funeral. I remember how lost she looked. She asked me that day, her eyes filled with tears, "Sammy, who's going to hold my hand now?" Struggling to hold back my tears. I told her, "I know it's not the same, but may I hold your hand?" She smiled a bit and said, "I would like that; I would like that very much." They had been holding hands for a lifetime, but now he was gone, and she seemed so lost. I was to visit her for the next several months, almost every day holding her hand and listening to the stories of her life with the man whom she knew loved her deeply. "He wasn't perfect," she said, "but his love for me was more than I could have ever dreamed of."

It was almost four months to the day when she passed away. She left a note for me that read, "My Dear Sammy, thank you for holding my hand."

I'm not sure why I'm sharing this story with you. I just feel a deep burden for those who haven't anyone to hold their hand. It must be very lonely to have no one hold your hand or share your struggles. But I sense the Spirit of God telling me that it is the church that must hold their hand and listen to their stories. It is not the role of the church to decide whose hand is worth holding and whose story is worth hearing.

Prayer Point
Lord, I pray for the church today, that she might have the courage to hold the hands and listen to the stories of those who are lost. Empower Your church to be love with skin on it.

WONDERING MOMENTS/QUESTIONS TO PONDER
(Read Proverbs 3:27.)

---

1. Over sixty years of marriage, and they were still holding hands! What does that image indicate concerning their relationship?

_____

_____

_____

_____

_____

2. Why do you think the lady felt lost when her husband died?

_____

_____

_____

_____

_____

3. Do you agree with the statement, "It's the role of the church to hold the hand and listen to the stories of those who seem lost? What hinders the church from fulfilling that role?

_____

_____

_____

_____

_____

65

THE WOODEN BOX

---◇---

"Let each of you look out not only for his own interests
but also for the interests of others" (Phil. 2:4).

I'm sitting in my office/man-cave reflecting, as I do every morning. On the mantle, there is a pine-scented candle burning, and in the fireplace, fire is glowing. I'm looking at a beautifully handcrafted tackle box that sits on the hearth. The tackle box was given to me by my dear friend, Delmas Jones. He gave it to me as a parting gift. On the inside of the box is a wooden bobber that was also hand-crafted by Delmas.

As I sit here in my rocking chair, admiring the wooden box, I realize how very blessed I am. I'm blessed this morning in knowing without a hint of doubt that I am loved! It's not always easy being a pastor. There will always be some who don't like you, but that is true for all of us. There will always be those who make our lives difficult. None of us are exempt from the experience of not being liked by everyone. However, knowing you are loved is a source of strength that enables you to move forward in life and not just sit and watch life pass by you!

On the inside of the wooden box, burned into the wood, is the stamped message, "Handcrafted by Delmas L. Jones." I think about the amount of time he spent crafting this beautiful gift, knowing that it was done as a labor of love. As difficult as life can sometimes be, it's important to remember that stamped upon each life is the message, "Handcrafted by God." We are all created by God and have a grand purpose to fulfill. That purpose is to tell those who pass our way that they are loved, to tell them they matter!

I have been so blessed in my life by those who have made it very clear that I matter and that I am loved. This morning, as I sit in my rocking chair, reflecting on the wooden box, I'm overwhelmed with a sense of gratitude. Still, I'm aware of those who don't feel as though they matter. They don't know how much God loves them.

So, today I will endeavor to tell them they matter and they are loved!

Prayer Point

Lord, thank you for loving me. Thank you for friends who let me know. Lead me to someone today who needs to hear the message of Your love for them.

WONDERING MOMENTS/QUESTIONS TO PONDER
(Read Philippians 2:4.)

———————◇———————

1. Looking out for the interest of others often means putting your interest aside. Why is it so difficult for us to put aside our self-interest?

   _____

   _____

   _____

   _____

   _____

2. Just as the wooden box was handcrafted with love, so you and I have been handcrafted by God! How does knowing that you have been created by God make you feel?

   _____

   _____

   _____

   _____

   _____

66

THERE IS ALWAYS A REASON TO SING

———————◇———————

"He who dwells in the secret place of the Most High shall abide under the shadow of the Almighty. I will say to the Lord, "He is my refuge and my fortress; My God, in Him, I will trust" (Ps. 91:1–2).

It was late, the kids were in bed asleep, and she sat at the kitchen table alone. Set in front of her was her Bible, the pages turned to Psalm 91, a cup of black coffee, and three stacks of bills. As she stared at the bills, tears streaming down her cheeks, as she began to pray, "Lord, You are my refuge and my fortress. You are my God, and in You, will I trust!"

With five children and very little money, she did the only thing she knew to do: pray! She prayed through the night. This night wasn't the first time she had been at the table, facing stacks of bills she couldn't pay, her heart filled with pain. However, this night would be different. Somehow, through the tears, and the sips of black coffee, and praying Psalm 91, she found new strength. Her heart overflowed with the assurance that she was not alone. Everything would be all right.

When morning came, she began cooking breakfast while singing the song, "Amazing Grace." For the one who perseveres in their faith, there is always a reason to sing!

Her children are now grown, and have become successful—with families of their own—and have strong faith! Life, at times, may seem very dark, but know this: for the one who believes, "Joy comes in the morning!"

Even if your tears are still falling and the coffee's grown cold, God's amazing grace, surrounds you and me, the morning will come, and you will sing again!

———————⋈———————

Prayer Point
Lord, You are my refuge and my fortress; I will trust in You. Lord, no matter what life may bring my way, help me to remember there is always a reason to sing. That reason is Your loving grace.

WONDERING MOMENTS/A
QUESTION TO PONDER
(Read Psalm 91:1–2.)

———————⋈———————

When life is complicated and even overwhelming, how can we still find a reason to sing?

_____

_____

_____

_____

_____

67

GRIPPED BY THE MASTER

————————⋈————————

"Fear not, for I am with you. Be not dismayed, for I am your God. I will strengthen you, yes, I will help you, I will uphold you, with My righteous right hand" (Isa. 41:10).

I love golf! There was a time when I played, at a minimum of twice a week. I wasn't half bad. I haven't played in quite a while for several reasons, but I still love the game. Some days, I'll see my bag sitting in the corner, and I will reach for a club and grip it.

There is one club in my bag I always seem to reach for—my One Iron. It's a great club that's very forgiving. By forgiving, I mean, you can mis-hit the ball and still find the fairway. MacGregor manufactured it. The shift is made of graphite and has a low bend point (a shaft designed to hit the ball high). It has a graphite face that helps with inertia at impact, giving the golfer greater distance. It also has a larger sweet spot, which means my swing doesn't have to be perfect to result in a decent shot. I love this club because it is easy to hit and very forgiving.

However, no matter how great the equipment one has, if one can't play, the best clubs in the world will be of no use. But when that same club is in the grip of a highly skilled player, great shots will be the result.

Now, what has all this to do with my life and your life? In whose grip is your life? You may be very gifted in many ways, but if your life is not in the hands of the Master, then your life will fail to have a positive impact on others. Your witness will be adverse.

The question we must answer is, Who is holding us? It makes all the difference in how impactful our life will be in the world. I want to be in the Master's grip. I want to be an instrument of His grace, skillfully used by Him to reveal the love and mercy He has for everybody.

Prayer Point
Lord, take hold of my life and make me an
instrument of Your strategic work in the world.
May I yield to Your grip in all things.

WONDERING MOMENTS/A QUESTION TO PONDER
(Read Isaiah 41:10.)

———————◦✕◦———————

Isaiah tells the people of God not to be afraid or dismayed. He says to them that God will strengthen them, help them, and uphold them with His righteous right hand. Can you think of a time when you experienced God's hand holding on to you?

_____

_____

_____

_____

_____

68

THE LIST

———————×———————

"Being confident of this very thing, that He who has begun a good work in you will complete it until the day of Jesus Christ" (Phil. 1:6).

We had been given an assignment by Pastor Jim who, at the time, was my then-fiancé and now my wife, Jennifer Willams pastor. We were going through premarital counseling. The assignment was simple, "I want both of you to take some time this week, and apart from each other, take a sheet of paper and list ten characteristics that reveal why you have chosen to marry this person. She and I were then to meet together and exchange our lists, sharing with the other what we had written. I remember him asking. "Of all the people in the world, why do you want to marry each other?"

I remember the night we met to exchange our lists. I handed her the list I had prepared, and she gave me the list she had written. We sat quietly, reading each other's list. It was an unforgettable moment for me. I never dreamed anyone could view me the way she did. I remember my eyes watering a bit. That list still humbles me. I review the list from time to time, and each time I'm convicted that I am not that man she once knew. But I want to be that man! I've had the list for some twenty-seven-plus years, and it still has the power to challenge me to be a better husband, father, son, and friend.

I think we often grow lazy or complacent in our relationships over time. Intimacy takes commitment. It takes devotion and dedication. It will be what we make of it. And, if we are to make it all that it can be, we must do more than making a list. We must fulfill this list. It is Christ who enables us to do so! I thank God that I have a wife who is long-suffering and full of grace. And I especially thank God that He hasn't given up on me. He has promised to complete the work He has begun in me!

———————⟨✕⟩———————

Prayer Point

Lord, I thank you for my wife who, after all this time, still believes in me. And Lord, I especially want to thank you for never giving up on me! I thank you that You will complete in me what You have begun!

WONDERING MOMENTS/QUESTIONS TO PONDER
(Read Philippians 1:6.)

———————◇———————

1. How confident are you that God will complete in you the work that He has begun?

_____

_____

_____

_____

_____

2. If we aren't careful, we can become complacent in our relationship with God. How can we avoid that complacency from occurring?

_____

_____

_____

_____

_____

3. Intimacy doesn't just happen. It takes commitment, devotion, and dedication. Take a moment and evaluate where you are in your loyalty and dedication to God.

_____

_____

_____

_____

_____

69

IS HE A DOG OR A RABBIT?

———————◇———————

"He who says he abides in Him ought himself also to walk just as He walked" (1 John 2:6).

The dog's name was Smokey, and the rabbit's name was Pepe; both belonged to my brother, Michael. We were living in an apartment in the small town of Fairburn, Georgia. The apartment was simple and not very large—there were seven of us living in a two-bedroom apartment. That's not counting Smokey and Pepe.

There were times when the dog and the rabbit were together, freely roaming the apartment. Now, Smokey was a puppy, and I suppose he was still trying to figure out his true identity, and on occasions became a bit confused. Smokey would follow after Pepe, hopping like a rabbit, rather than walking or running like a dog. It was something to watch and a source of laughter for us. Just imagine, a dog thinking himself to be a rabbit—how funny!

What's not so funny is to exert a lot of time and energy trying to be someone that you aren't. I've known people like that, and I'm sure you have as well. Maybe we've been guilty of it ourselves.

The point is, no matter how skilled Smokey became at hopping like a rabbit, he would never be a rabbit. Likewise, no matter how hard a person works at being Christian, unless their faith in Christ has transformed them, they are not Christian. They may be religious, but being religious (doing) is not the same as having a relationship with Christ (being). It's not about acting like a Christian; instead, it is about *being a Christian.*

Take a moment and reflect. Ask yourself, "Am I really a Christian? Have I yielded to the Lordship of Christ? Or am I still trying to live as a Christian in my strength?

Remember, it's not about doing—it's about being!

Prayer Point
Lord, You have called me to be in a relationship with You. Keep me from being caught up in acting like a Christian and lead me to be Christian. Help not confuse being religious with being authentically Christian.

WONDERING MOMENTS/QUESTIONS TO PONDER
(Read 1 John 2:6.)

1. Have you at times tried to be someone that you're not to impress someone?

   _____

2. If you have, you are certainly not alone. But, think for a moment, why was it so important to try to be someone that you aren't?

   _____

   _____

   _____

   _____

3. Is there a difference between "doing" and "being"? And, if so, what is it?

   _____

   _____

   _____

   _____

   _____

70

LITTLE SAMMY

———✗———

*"But now, thus says the Lord, who created you, O Jacob,
and He who formed you, O Israel: "Fear not, for I
have redeemed you; I have called you by your name;
You are Mine" (Isa 43:1).*

It was given to me by my home church some fifty years ago. I was entering the third grade, and Fairburn United Methodist Church had a tradition of giving those entering the third grade a Bible. The Bible sits in my office prominently displayed. I love that Bible. It has been a source of encouragement, a reminder that I have been loved and nurtured by a community of people called the church.

On the cover of the Bible, a bit faded now, is engraved my name. I remember being very persistent that my full name, Samuel Edward Wilder, Jr., be on the cover. My pastor, Reverend Grady Lively, assured me that it would be. But, when I received the Bible, the name printed was Sammy, not Samuel. I remember being upset, although my pastor and others called me "Little Sammy."

Today, however, when I look at that Bible and see the faded name Sammy E Wilder, Jr., my heart is warmed, and I know that

I've been loved and nurtured by so many. I want you to know today that God knows your name, and He loves you very much!

———————⟨×⟩———————

Prayer Point

Lord, You know my name. You know everything about me. And still, You love me! I thank you, Lord, for Your church. Empower the church in these days to claim her true identity and fulfill her divine destiny.

WONDERING MOMENTS/QUESTIONS TO PONDER
(Read Isaiah 43:1.)

———◇———

1. What does it mean to be redeemed?

_____

_____

_____

_____

_____

2. Knowing that God knows you by name, does that encourage you? Why or why not?

_____

_____

_____

_____

_____

3. If you belong to God, what does that mean for your life in this world?

_____

_____

_____

_____

_____

71

WHO SETS YOUR AGENDA?

———————◇———————

"In all your ways acknowledge Him, and He shall direct your paths" (Prov. 3:6).

The old pastor asked his young student, "Is there smoke in the chimney?" He then proceeded to share a bit of wisdom with the young student. "I want a pastor who gets up early and spends time in the Word of God and prayer for the people he serves." The young student was feeling pretty proud of himself because he did get up early each morning.

The old pastor continued, "Nothing must get in the way of one's morning time with God." A sudden conviction came over the young student. Yes, he did get up early, and yes, he did read his Bible and prayed. But, the truth is that those early mornings were often spent going over his day planner. To be honest, he spent more time looking at his day planner than he did reading the Word or praying.

The old pastor continued as if reading the young student's mind, "Son, you must never be a servant with an open day planner and a closed Bible. Never let your day planner suffocate your Bible. It's a good thing to be organized and have a schedule for your day. But, your agenda must never supersede God's agenda.

"You must never allow your day planner to dictate your day. God's Spirit must always lead you. There will be times when your day planner and God's plans don't coincide. In those moments, follow God's leading and not your day planner."

Prayer Point

Lord, it's true that prior planning prevents poor performance. Yet, Lord, I know there are times when what I have on my schedule for the day may not always be in keeping with Your plans. May I always be subject to Your Holy Spirit and lay aside my to-do list and, without hesitation, follow You!

WONDERING MOMENTS/QUESTIONS TO PONDER
(Read Proverbs 3:6.)

———————✂———————

1. What are some of the ways you might acknowledge God in your daily life?

   _____

   _____

   _____

   _____

   _____

2. While day-planners are an excellent tool for organizing our day, how can they become a hindrance in our obeying God?

   _____

   _____

   _____

   _____

   _____

72

THROW IT OUT!

———— ∝ ————

"For we are to God, the fragrance of Christ among those who are being saved and among those who are perishing" (2 Cor. 2:15).

The smell was horrible. It was sickening. Everyone was trying to figure out where the smell was coming from, and I wasn't talking. I knew what was causing the offensive odor. The smell was coming from my bag. Our den leader pulled the van off the road and instructed us to get out. She then began to look through each bag. The search didn't take long. I remember her opening my bag and almost passing out.

There it was, wrapped up in a paper towel—a small dead brim. I shouldn't have kept it, but I did. I wanted to show it to my mom. It was the first fish I had ever caught. I remember our leader telling me, "Sammy, the fish has got to go," and she threw the small lifeless brim as far as she could away from the van.

The point of the story is, and there is a point; there are sometimes things we are holding on to that need to be thrown out. I'm not talking about material things but rather habits or patterns in our life that need to go. Our lives should be as a sweet-smelling offering unto the Lord. Read Psalm 139:4 and 2 Corinthians 2:15 and think about it.

So, whatever is stinking up the "van of your life" throw it out! Today!

———————————⋈———————————

Prayer Point

Lord, by Your Spirit, reveal those areas of my life that dishonor You. Lord, whatever it takes for me to become as a sweet-smelling offering unto You, do it! Lord, I want my life to bear witness to Your presence living in me.

WONDERING MOMENTS/QUESTIONS TO PONDER
(Read 2 Corinthians 2:15.)

————————⟨✕⟩————————

1. Have you ever smelled an unpleasant odor?

_____

2. What makes our life a sweet fragrance to God?

_____

_____

_____

_____

_____

3. Are there areas in your life that are producing an offensive odor before God? If so, what should you do about it?

_____

_____

_____

_____

_____

73

KEEP ON STEPPING

———◦———

"But those who wait on the Lord shall renew their strength; they shall mount up with wings like eagles. They shall run and not be weary. They shall walk and not faint" (Isa. 40:31).

I saiah 40:31 is one of my favorite verses in all of scripture. It's such an encouraging verse. I don't know about you, but for me, there are seasons in my faith journey when I need encouragement. The walk of faith is not an easy one to make. You don't just walk down the aisle, shake the preacher's hand, pray a prayer, and then coast your way to heaven. The successful walk of faith requires patience, determination, and a resolute spirit. The journey may begin by taking that first step, but it doesn't end there. Our walk of faith is a lifelong journey with peaks and valleys. But knowing that we don't walk alone is a source of encouragement.

Life may indeed have its ups and downs, but by trusting in the Lord and following after Him, taking one step and then another and another, we will overcome every obstacle in our faith journey!

No matter how hard your journey of faith may seem today, just keep stepping—putting one foot in front of the other—as you follow Jesus. Don't give up, and you'll make it!

Remember, the journey of faith is accomplished one step at a time— so let's keep stepping!

———————✕———————

Prayer Point
Lord, there are times when the journey is hard and the temptation to turn back is strong. Lord, grant me the strength and courage to press on, knowing that You are with me and leading me.

WONDERING MOMENTS/QUESTIONS TO PONDER
(Read Isaiah 40:31.)

———————⌖———————

1. What does it mean to wait on the Lord?

_____

_____

_____

_____

_____

2. Are there things you can do while waiting on God? Name some.

_____

_____

_____

_____

_____

3. When you grow weary, what do you tend to do? What should you do?

_____

_____

_____

_____

_____

74

STOP THROWING CLUBS

———————✕———————

"Therefore bear fruits worthy of repentance"
(Matt. 3:8).

Many of you are familiar with the prayer written by American theologian, Reinhold Niebuhr, commonly referred to as The Serenity Prayer. It is a prayer I've prayed many times over the years. "God, grant me the serenity to accept the things I cannot change, the courage to change the things I can, and the wisdom to know the difference." (Sifton, 2004). The prayer intends to bring peace, faith, and certainty to the mind and heart of those seeking God's support.

One of my favorite coffee, mugs, is one given to me by my wife, Jennifer. On the of the cup is the phrase Born to Golf. On the back is the golfer's Serenity Prayer. "God grant me the serenity to accept the shots I miss, the courage never to give up, and the wisdom not to throw my clubs in the water."

While there is a bit of humor in the golfer's serenity prayer, there is a message to be pondered. How do I react when things in life go wrong? When circumstances are not what I would have them to be, due to choices I've made or maybe decisions others have made that have negatively impacted my life, how do I respond?

As a Christian, my response to such things should be one that reveals Christ to those around me. I confess, however, my reaction is not always Christlike. There are times when anger controls my response, resulting in a compounding of the problem rather than its resolution.

Our response to adversity significantly impacts our witness. In those moments, we either reveal the fruit of the Holy Spirit or the fruit of our flesh. *Oh, and stop throwing your clubs in the water—Sam!*

Prayer Point
Lord, when adversity arises in my life, may I rely on Your Spirit, who dwells in me to guide me in my response so others will see Your character through my actions and attitudes. May my witness be effectual in bringing others to know You as both Savior and Lord.

WONDERING MOMENTS/A QUESTION TO PONDER
(Read Matthew 3:8.)

———————◇———————

Life is filled with adversity. What are some ways you might react that would reveal to others your faith in Christ?

_____

_____

_____

_____

_____

75

MISPLACED PRIORITIES

————————⋊————————

"But seek first the kingdom of God and His Righteousness, and all these things shall be added to you" (Matt. 6:33).

I t was Sunday morning, and the service had gone well. After the worship service, I did what I always did—stood at the door and greeted the people as they left. I noticed a young couple standing off to the side, who had been visiting the church for several Sundays but had not joined. I remember walking over to the couple and telling them how glad I was to see them back, and as I was speaking to them, my wife Jennifer, who was pregnant at the time with our first child, Garrett, came up and tapped me on the shoulder and said, "I need to tell you something." I replied, "Okay, just give me a moment, and I'll be right with you." I then turned back to the young couple who were expressing interest in joining the church. Again Jennifer tapped me on the shoulder and said, "I need to tell you something now!"

Here I am a young pastor talking to prospective members, and my wife is demanding my attention. I was a bit annoyed. I told the couple to give me a moment, and I then turned my focus to Jennifer and said, "What is it!" She whispered in my ear, "My water just broke, and we need to go." At that point, I forgot all about the young couple and took

Jennifer to the car and then remembered, wait a minute, this is a new car, I don't want the seat to get stained. So, I told her to wait while I went to find a towel to put on the seat where she would be riding.

Here is my wife pregnant with our first child, her water has broken, and I'm worried about having my car seat stained. We did have to travel from Kings Bay to the hospital in Brunswick, and I'm insistent on protecting my car seat?

I remember Jennifer waiting, as I found a towel, placed it on her seat and then, and only then, did I let her sit in the car! We made it to the hospital, and some twenty hours later, Garrett was born. Reflecting, I admit that maybe I had misplaced my priorities. I seemed more concerned about the car than the fact that my wife was in labor, and our firstborn was on the way.

Misplaced priorities—have you experienced them? They can be dangerous. As a pastor, I have seen when the church has focused on the wrong things. And, the result has almost always been negative. And in my life, I've experienced negative consequences because of misplaced priorities.

The church has two priorities: to love God and to love people! The truth is, sometimes doing so gets messy, and we don't have time to wait for a "towel of protection." We need to go and just do it! Don't allow your desire to keep away from the mess of life prevent you from doing what needs doing right now—love God and love people, even when doing so is messy! Just do it!

———————$\propto$———————

Prayer Point
Lord, it is so easy in today's world to get off track. Lord, may I stay in Your Word and follow Your ways. May Your priorities become mine, and may I continue to grow and mature in the faith.

WONDERING MOMENTS/QUESTIONS TO PONDER
(Read Matthew 6:33)

1. How do you define the word priority?

_____

_____

_____

_____

_____

2. Have you ever had your priorities in the wrong order?

_____

3. List the priorities of your life in the order of importance to you.

_____

_____

_____

_____

_____

76

THE RIVER OF GOD'S LOVE

———————⋉———————

"Jesus answered and said to her, 'Whoever drinks of this water will thirst again, but whoever drinks of the water that I shall give him will never thirst. But the water that I shall give him will become in him a fountain of water springing up into everlasting life'" *(John 4:13–14).*

In a small Samaritan village called Sychar, there was a woman who had been married five times, and now she was living with a man that wasn't her husband. She came to draw water from the old well. Little did she know that she would have a life-changing encounter with a Jew named Jesus. It was about noon when Jesus arrived at the old well. He and his disciples were returning to Galilee from the Judean countryside. The disciples had gone into town to buy food, and Jesus remained alone at the well.

Most of the village women came early in the morning to draw water from the well when it wasn't so hot. But this woman came at noon to avoid the others because, to them, she was an outcast. She was the subject of their gossip and ridicule. Her's was a broken and lonely life.

Jesus, tired and thirsty from his journey, asked the woman for a drink of water from the well. The woman was caught off-guard because Jesus was a Jew and she was a Samaritan woman—Jews and Samaritans had no dealings with each other. Yet, Jesus asks her for a drink. She questioned Jesus, asking why. His reply would change her life forever. "If you knew how generous God is and who I am, you would ask me for living water, and I would give you water, and you would never thirst again." The woman said, "Give me a drink of your water so I'll never have to come here again. Jesus began to tell the woman all about her life.

She believed that day in the love of God and that God's love was for her. She said yes that day to God's love, and her life was forever changed. Her life was changed because she encountered a Jew named Jesus, who looked beyond her sin and saw her pain. He looked beyond the social norms of His day and gave God's love away.

I love the song, "There is a River." One verse in particular stands out for me. "There came a thirsty woman; she was drawing from a well. You see her life was ruined and wasted, and her soul was bound for hell. Oh, but then she met the Master who told of her great sin. He said, if you drink of this water, you'll never thirst again." The chorus says, "There is a river that flows from deep within. There is a fountain that frees the soul from sin. Come to these waters, for there is a vast supply. There is a river that never shall run dry." (Sapp, 1969).

There are so many like this woman. Their lives are broken and in ruin, and they need to drink from the fountain of God's love. We are called to share that love with others—even those who are the subject of disgrace and rejection. I'm forced this morning to ask myself how often have I passed by broken and lonely people in need of God's love. God, forgive me and open my eyes to those who come to the well at noon—the outcast and talked about—and may I dare to share from the fountain of Your love that never shall run dry.

———————◇———————

Prayer Point

Lord, I confess there are days when I act as though I am the only one You love. Forgive me for closing my eyes to the broken and lonely, the outcast, and the shamed. I pray that Your love would be in me a wellspring springing up and overflowing into the lives of those around me.

WONDERING MOMENTS/QUESTIONS TO PONDER
(Read John 4:13–14.)

1. Name a time when you were extremely thirsty?

_____

_____

_____

_____

_____

2. How did you feel when you were able to finally drink some water?

_____

_____

3. What did Jesus mean when He said, "Whoever drinks of the water I shall give will never thirst"?

_____

_____

_____

_____

_____

77

WHEN STORMS ARE RAGING

———————∝———————

"Now it happened, on a certain day, that He got into a boat with His disciples. And He said to them, 'Let us cross over to the other side of the lake.' And they launched out. But as they sailed, He fell asleep. And a windstorm came down on the lake, and they were filling with water and were in jeopardy. And they came to Him and awoke Him, saying, 'Master, Master, we are perishing!' Then He arose and rebuked the wind and the raging of the water, and there was a calm. But He said to them, 'Where is your faith?' And they were afraid, and marveled, saying to one another, 'Who can this be? For He commands even the winds and water, and they obey Him!'" (Luke 8:22–25)

One day Jesus and his disciples got into a boat to get to the other side of the lake. The water was as smooth as glass, and the sun was bright in the sky overhead. It was a beautiful day. It wasn't long before Jesus fell asleep, resting peacefully in the front of the boat.

All was going well, but suddenly, out of nowhere, a storm came upon them. The sky darkened, the winds blew forcefully, and the water began pouring into the boat. All the while, Jesus slept undisturbed by the raging storm. But not the disciples; they were in full panic mode. Just a few minutes earlier, everything was beautiful, and the next, they feared for their very lives.

Life can be that way sometimes. The storms of life can seem to appear out of nowhere. What do you do when the storms of life begin to blow, and you suddenly find yourself overwhelmed?

Back to the story: the disciples wake Jesus up and shout, "Master, we are going down!" Jesus stood up and commanded the wind to stop and the lake to be still, and suddenly all was peaceful again!

Now, again the question—What do we do when the storms of life suddenly appear in our lives? The story reveals some answers. Notice that Jesus was in the boat with the disciples. When the rain came, the disciples were with Jesus! Is Jesus in your life? Next, notice that Jesus wasn't intimidated by the situation; He was at peace. When life becomes a storm, remember Jesus, the Prince of peace, is with you. Notice what the disciples did. They cried out to Jesus for help. When faced with difficult situations, do you try to handle them in your strength and wisdom, or do you trust Jesus?

In each of our lives, there will be stormy times, and there will be overwhelming moments when all seems out of control. I want to declare to you today that if Jesus is in your life, there is no need to fear. He will see you through the storm. The wind and sea of trouble will not overtake you! Being aware of God's sovereignty and yielding our lives to His care ensures victory over the storm we may be facing or will face.

———————⋈———————

Prayer Point
*Lord, I pray for Your peace when the storms rage
and life seems overwhelming, may I trust in You.*

WONDERING MOMENTS/A QUESTION TO PONDER
(Read Luke 8:22–25.)

———◇———

Amid the storm, Jesus was at peace, but the disciples feared for their lives. How might you live at peace in the storms of your life?

_____

_____

_____

_____

_____

78

DON'T SETTLE

———◇———

"And throwing aside his garment, he rose and came to Jesus. So Jesus answered and said to him, 'What do you want Me to do for you?' The blind man said to Him, 'Rabboni that I may receive my sight.' Then Jesus said to him, Go your way; your faith has made you well.' And immediately, he received his sight and followed Jesus on the road" (Mark 10:50–52).

He was sitting in the same spot he had been sitting for what seemed to be forever. He was blind and had been for a very long time. Jesus and His disciples had been spending some time in town, and as they were leaving, with a crowd of people escorting them, the blind man overheard the name, Jesus. He had heard that Jesus could heal people. The blind man thought, *Maybe Jesus might be willing to heal even me.* With all the courage he could muster, he called out, "Have mercy on me! Please, Son of David, have mercy on me." The crowd around told him to be quiet. But he had spent a lifetime being quiet. Not today, not at this moment; he refused and shouted even louder, "Sir, Please have mercy on me!"

Jesus shouted, "Come!" The man threw off his coat and stood to his feet and stumbled his way toward Jesus. As he stood in front of Jesus, still blind and unable to see. "Sir," he said, when asked by Jesus what it was he wanted, "I want to see!" With that, Jesus healed his sight, and the man followed Jesus as He left the town.

This story is one of my favorites in the Bible. There are a couple of things in the story I want you to notice. First, the blind man refused to be silenced by the others. He was determined. How often have we been silent when we should have been shouting? How many times have we allowed Jesus to pass through our situation, and paralyzed by fear, we've remained in the same place we've been for so long—when we could have moved on to better things. How often have we held on to the "coat of the familiar" and missed a new vision? Often in our addiction to being comfortable, our willingness to settle in our same old spot along the roadside, we've missed seeing all that God would have us see and experience in life.

Like the blind man, aren't you tired of sitting along the roadside as the world passes? Maybe it's time to shout rather than be silent. Perhaps it's time to throw off the familiar and go after the spectacularly unfamiliar! The point is Jesus is always passing through your Jericho, and He's always saying come. The question is, are you and I willing, and will we respond? Be careful how you answer because having your eyes opened and following after Jesus will mean leaving your familiar spot for something new and unfamiliar. But unfamiliar things can mean for us newfound freedom to live a life of purpose! Remember, Jesus is always passing through your Jericho. Don't just settle—shout! Don't hold on to the familiar because it makes you comfortable. Follow after Jesus and see where the road might lead!

———————∝———————

Prayer Point
Lord, don't let me grow complacent in my faith.
Don't allow me to settle for something because
it is comfortable and familiar. Stir in me, oh
Lord, a passion for following You wherever that
might lead.

WONDERING MOMENTS/QUESTIONS TO PONDER
(Read Mark 10:50–53.)

———————⋈———————

1. When the crowd told the blind man to be quiet, what was his response?

   _____

   _____

   _____

   _____

   _____

2. What do you think the symbolism is in the blind man throwing aside his garment before coming to Jesus?

   _____

   _____

   _____

   _____

   _____

3. Once healed, what did the man do?

_____

_____

_____

_____

_____

79

I SHOT MY GRANDMOTHER

———◇———

"But why do you call me 'Lord, Lord, and not do the things which I say?'" (Luke 6:46).

I shot my grandmother! I didn't mean to do it. It just happened. I was sitting in the living room, holding my new BB gun. It was an awesome gun. My dad had given it to me. It looked just like his 30/30 Winchester. I don't think I had put the gun down since I had gotten it as a gift. I loved that gun.

My grandmother (Big Grandmama) was in the kitchen. She had told me several times to put the gun away or take it outside. Well, I didn't. I didn't put it away or take it out to play. I remember shaking the gun back and forth and telling her, "See, it's empty—no BBs." She said, "Put the gun away, or go outside!"

When she returned to the kitchen, which was, by the way, two rooms over, I remember cocking the rifle, pointing it at the wall, and that's when it happened, I pulled the trigger. To my horrified surprise, a BB went flying bouncing off one wall and then another and another and, believe it or not, made its way into the kitchen, hitting my grandmother in the leg. I remember hearing her scream.

"What did I tell you! Give me the gun!" And with that, she took my gun, and I didn't see it again for several weeks.

I didn't mean to shoot my grandmother. It was an accident. No, it wasn't; it was the result of rebellion. It was the result of not heeding her warning. It was selfish. I wanted to hold my gun, and I wanted to pull the trigger. I didn't want to shoot Big Grandmama, but I did. It happened because I refused to listen.

I would like to say that was the only time I failed to heed the wisdom of another or a warning from someone, but it's not. I've done it plenty. Maybe you have as well. I don't mean you shot your grandmother, but you failed to heed the warning that there was a danger in your actions.

As Christians, we're taught that there are dangers in not obeying God. There is danger in living life on our terms, doing what we want and when we want. Be careful to be a doer of His Word and not a hearer only. The result will be a good and blessed life!

———————◇———————

Prayer Point
Lord, may I be careful to walk in obedience to You!

WONDERING MOMENTS/QUESTIONS TO PONDER
(Read Luke 6:46.)

———————∝———————

1. My grandmother had warned me. Yet, I refused to listen. What was at the root of my disobedience?

_____

_____

_____

_____

_____

2. Disobedience has consequences. Does it mean that God no longer loves you when you are disciplined?

_____

_____

_____

_____

_____

80

WHEN BEING RIGHT IS WRONG

————————⚓————————

"Therefore, as the elect of God, holy and beloved, put on tender mercies, kindness, humility, meekness, longsuffering; bearing with one another, and forgiving one another, if anyone has a complaint against another; even as Christ forgave you, so you also must do. But above all these things put on love, which is the bond of perfection. And let the peace of God rule in your hearts, to which also you were called in one body, and be thankful" (Col. 3:12–15).

"Sam, you're right. You're right about our policy concerning behavior." That's what he said, as I sat in his office. I was there because a parent had complained about a decision I had made concerning the parent's son.

As I sat there, I remember thinking, "Yeah, you bet I'm right, so what am I doing sitting here?" I felt like a student sitting in the principal's office! I was mad, and Pastor Ligon knew it. We sat there in silence for a long time. The longer I sat there, the angrier I became. *I don't have time for this,* I thought. *I'm not changing my mind. I'm right, and you know it!* I thought.

I was fuming while Pastor Ligon remained calm. He finally broke the awkward silence by repeating. "Sam, you're right." There was a short pause, and I remember he asked me to look at him; I was looking down at the time, staring at the floor to hide my frustration. I slowly lifted my head and looked him in the eyes, and suddenly realized this godly man was for me and not against me. It was then the lesson began with a question. "Sam, you are right about the policy, but I wonder if there is ever a time when being 'right' is 'wrong.'" What? He continued, "Sam, there is a right way and wrong way to be right. Your 'rightness' is wrong because it lacks compassion! You're a gifted leader, but sometimes you exercise that gift apart from the Holy Spirit's control. When that happens, you lose your effectiveness. I believe in you, Sam," he said, "I just want you to be right the right way!" He then prayed for me and asked me to pray for him.

When I left his office, I wasn't angry; I left feeling blessed and built up! I had just been admonished yet encouraged. Pastor Ligon was right—the right way. I remember thinking, *Lord, I want to be like that*! There would be more lessons to come, and I am grateful for each one!

Prayer Point
Lord, in all things, may I be a person of compassion, and may I be right the right way!

WONDERING MOMENTS/QUESTIONS TO PONDER
(Read Colossians 3:12–15.)

————————⊂×————————

1. Think about a time when you were right, and you knew it, but your attitude was not right.

_____

_____

_____

2. Have you ever experienced correction from a superior and left feeling uplifted?

_____

_____

3. How would you answer the question? Is there ever a time when being "right" is "wrong"?

_____

_____

_____

_____

_____

81

PLAYING CHICKEN WITH THE COWS

———————◇———————

"Be still, and know that I am God. I will be exalted
among the nations. I will be exalted in the earth! The
Lord of hosts is with us. The God of Jacob is our refuge"
(Ps. 46:10–11).

It was my first time on a go-cart. It belonged to my friend, Andrew.
I remember being so excited. Andrew's dad showed me how to
operate the go-cart. I had this—no problem—or so I thought. I
soon stepped on the gas, and it was on! I was riding in the pasture
behind their house, and in the field, there were cows, a lot of cows.
They were everywhere. It seemed as though one cow was making
it her life's goal to get in my way. If I turned right to avoid her, she
turned right to get in my way. If I turned left, the same thing; she
turned left, staying in the way. I remember thinking, *Okay, cow, it's
on*! I decided to stop trying to avoid the cow, and I headed straight
for her at full speed!

There I was, eight years old, playing chicken with a cow! I hate
to admit it, but the cow won. I turned at the last minute as the cow
stood her ground. The truth is I forgot where the brakes were. The

adventure came to a stop finally when I remembered to put my foot on the brake peddle. That would be the first and last time I was allowed to drive Andrew's go-cart!

It's funny to think about now, but at that moment I was terrified. It seemed that no matter which way I turned, the cow was determined to get in the way. Life can be that way. We're traveling along the path of life, and it seems that no matter which way we turn, an obstacle stands in our way. I've learned over the years that the answer is not to play chicken with your life but to stop—Just put your foot on the brake and pray, and God will direct your path. God will help you to avoid the obstacles that stand in your way.

So, if you are facing obstacles on every side, the answer is not to play chicken but to stop and pray, and God will show you the way! Remember, stop playing chicken and start praying for wisdom! God, who knows what is best for you, will show you what to do and which way to turn.

Oh, and stop trying to run over the cow and put the brakes on!

———————◇———————

Prayer Point
Lord, I know I tend to charge forward without
always thinking it through or hearing from You.
Lord, I recommit my life to You and Your ways.
Lead me by Your Spirit, Lord, so that in all things,
I may honor You.

WONDERING MOMENTS/QUESTIONS TO PONDER
(Read Psalm 46:10–11.)

———————⟨×⟩———————

1. Why is it so hard to be still in our daily life?

_____

_____

_____

_____

_____

2. What is often the result of charging forward without first seeking God?

_____

_____

_____

_____

_____

3. The Psalmist refers to God as his refuge. What does he mean?

_____

_____

_____

_____

_____

82

A SACK FULL OF MANGOS

———————∝———————

"As you, therefore, have received Christ Jesus the Lord, so walk in Him, rooted and built up in Him and established in the faith, as you have been taught, abounding in it with thanksgiving" (Col. 2:6–7).

It was the fifth day the young boy had brought me a bag full of mangos. Don't get me wrong; I love mangos, but a person can only eat so many before they begin to affect your bodily functions. Sorry, but it's true. I was with a mission team serving in the Blue Mountains of Jamaica, in a community called Williams Field.

The team would visit homes during the day, sharing the Good News of Jesus Christ, and at night, we would gather with the community for a time of worship. Our first night, a young boy came down to the altar during the invitation and gave his heart to Jesus. I remember thinking, *I'm not sure he knows what he's doing, he's so young.* After speaking with him for a few minutes, I realized he was serious about committing to follow Jesus. So, we prayed, and he asked Jesus to come into his heart and to be the Lord of his life. It was a great moment. The service ended, and I was tired and, I'm sorry to say, more interested in going to bed then talking to people.

The next morning, the young boy showed up at the door of the home where other members of the team and I were staying. In his arms was a bag full of mangos. He asked the lady of the house if I could come to the door. "He's not awake," the lady replied. "I'll wait for him," the young boy said, and he did. I finally got up and dressed and went outside to find the boy waiting for me with a bag full of mangos. He handed them to me and said, "These are for you" and quickly ran away. The next morning the same thing, and the next and the next. I love mangos, but I was beginning to dislike them.

It was the fifth morning of mangos, and I didn't want to be ungrateful but, *Enough with the mangos*, I thought. I remember asking the boy, "Why do you keep bringing me mangos?" He replied, "Because I love Jesus, and you love mangos." I told him, "Yes, I do like mangos, but I think I have enough. You don't have to bring me any more." I will never forget what this little boy said to me: "Sir, it is the only thing I have to give to say thank you for giving me Jesus." I asked, "Where do you get these mangos?" He pointed and told me, "From those trees. I climb them because the best ones are at the top. And I want you to have the best." Well, to make a long story less long. I gladly received a bag full of mangos every morning for ten days, each time saying, "Thank you," and the little boy saying, "Thank you for sharing Jesus with me!"

I learned something over those two weeks. I learned the meaning of gratitude. Gratitude is more than saying thank you and walking away. Gratitude is the outward expression of an overflowing heart! Just think, a little boy climbing a tree to pick mangos to give to someone he didn't really know, wanting only to express his thankfulness. Oh, and some of those trees were around 130 feet high.

As much as I tried, I couldn't eat all those mangos, so I shared with the other members of the team. But isn't that how genuine gratitude operates? The grateful heart overflowing with thanksgiving seeks continually to express in actions what words alone cannot convey. Remember, a life of gratitude is not so much about saying thank you as it is about *living out your thank you*!

Is our thankfulness expressed in mere words, or do our actions speak it? Think about it; it's worth pondering,

———————✕———————

Prayer Point

Lord, let my life be lived in a continual state of thankfulness, not only in the words I speak but in the way I live. May I always be mindful that You have redeemed me! And because of that truth, my whole life should be an act of praise and thanksgiving!

WONDERING MOMENTS/QUESTIONS TO PONDER
(Read Colossians 2:6–7.)

———————⚬———————

1. Why did the young boy continue to bring me mangos every morning?

   _____

   _____

   _____

   _____

   _____

2. Genuine gratitude is more than just saying thank you. How would you describe a life of genuine gratitude?

   _____

   _____

   _____

   _____

   _____

3. What would life look like if the church lived in a continual state of thankfulness?

_____

_____

_____

_____

_____

83

JOY

But the anointing which you have received from Him abides in you, and you do not need that anyone teach you; but as the same anointing teaches you concerning all things, and is true, and is not a lie, and just as it has taught you, you will abide in Him. (1 John 2:27)

Her name suited her, Joy. Joy never seemed to be in a bad mood. She just seemed always to smile. This time would be no different, even though she was very sick and lying in a hospital room at Emory University.

We were on our way to a Men's gathering in Atlanta, Georgia. There would be thousands who would gather. The conference was a part of the Promise Keepers Movement, and we were excited to be going. There were six of us in all. We had been on a journey of discipleship for some time. As we were leaving Blackshear, I asked the men if they minded taking a little time to stop by the Emory University Medical Center, so we might pray for Joy, who was the sister of my good friend Mark. To the man, each of them said they didn't mine. None of us was prepared for what would happen that day.

We soon arrived at the hospital and made our way to Joy's room. She looked tired. Her mom was sitting in the chair next to the window adjacent to the bed. On the walls, written on paper, were Scriptures that spoke of healing and faith in God. There were a couple of bibles in the room; both were opened and turned to passages on healing. As we entered the room, all six of us felt it. It was strange and compelling. We didn't know what it was; we just knew that it was there, and we were being affected. Never-the-less, we washed our hands, and each of the men introduced themselves. There was some small nervous talk for a few minutes. I then asked if we could pray for her, with a smile, she said, "sure, I would like that." I don't know why, but I was finding it hard to pray because of the unusual feeling, or maybe a better description would be presence. I stumbled through the prayer, asking God to heal Joy and to restore her to perfect health, a prayer I'm sure had been prayed over her many times.

When I finished praying, she and her mom both said thank you. We were about to leave the room when it happened – Something that would impact all six of us in a life-altering way. Joy, pushing herself up, asked if she might pray for us. "Yes, of course, please do, we need it." And with that, Joy began to pray. Oh my! something was happening to all six of us, as Joy, in a soft, quiet voice, prayed.

We had come to pray for her, and we had come to minister to her. But as she prayed, it hit me what the strange and unusual, for me and the other five, present, was – it was the anointing. Though her voice was weak and soft, there was a power in her words! We left as different men. We had been changed somehow. We were quiet for a while. It just wasn't the time for small talk when something so powerful had just happened.

We went on to the Promise Keepers gathering. We listened to men of God like T.D. Jakes and Tony Evans and coach Bill McCartney. Don't get me wrong; they were great, and being with thousands of men, all of whom were seeking God, was indeed a fantastic experience. But for the six of us, who had encountered a young woman of faith, named Joy, the conference couldn't hold a candle to the blaze we had experienced in that hospital room.

Our lives were different, not because of 50,000 men gathered together to worship and pray, but our lives were changed because we had experienced the quiet whispered power of God's anointed child named Joy! The anointing of God, the presence of God, will break you. Fifty Thousand men, cheering and singing, as great as it was, didn't hold a candle to the anointed child of God in room 506. I want you to know today that as God's child yielded to His Sovereign power, you can profoundly affect those around you!

————————⟨✕⟩————————

Prayer Point
Lord, I pray that Your anointing might rest upon me. I pray that as I yield to Your Lordship, others would experience Your presence and would be forever changed.

WONDERING MOMENTS/QUESTIONS TO PONDER
(Read 1 John 2: 27.)

1. What does it mean to abide?

_____

_____

_____

_____

2. What was the unusual presence in the room?

_____

_____

_____

_____

3. What role did Scripture play in Joy's healing?

_____

_____

_____

_____

_____

ABOUT THE AUTHOR

————⟨×⟩————

Sam Wilder is a gifted teacher and preacher, dedicated to sharing the good news of God's grace to a broken and hurting world. He has served as a pastor, evangelist, missionary, and Christian school administrator for over thirty years. He has witnessed what this message of grace can do in the lives of people.

It is the passion of Sam's life to be used by God in encouraging, motivating, and equipping local churches as they seek to become strategic centers of God's grace.

He is a graduate of Georgia Southern University and Candler School of Theology at Emory University. He is married to Jennifer, and they have four children: Garrett, Cole, Aaron, and Kayla.

In 2017, Sam was diagnosed with Parkinson's Disease, and though some days are a struggle, he continues to find new ways to fulfill his passion for sharing the good news of God's grace with others.

BIBLIOGRAPHY

Bowden, Tripp. *Freddie and Me*. Skyhorse Publishing, New York, New York, 2009.

Brown, Dr. Mike. *Avoiding The Snare*. Diamond Publishing, Mobile, Alabama, 2007.

Dunnam, Maxie. *The Workbook on Abiding in Christ: The Way of Living Prayer*. The Upper Room, Nashville, Tennessee, 2010.

Dickson, John. *Humilitas*. Zondervan, Grand Rapids, Michigan, 2011.

Ellis, Linda. "The Dash." 1996, *Southwestern Inspire Kindness Inc. thedashpoem.com*, 2020

Farr, Bob. *Renovate Or Die*. Abingdon Press, Nashville, Tennessee, 2011.

Hodges, Chris. *Fresh Air*. Tyndale Momentum, Tulsa, Oklahoma, 2012.

Holley, Al. "Come Next Spring." *Friends Like You*. Twelve Oaks Studios, Marietta, Georgia, 1980, Vinyl LP Album.

Kendall, R.T. *Controlling The Tongue*. Charisma House, Lake Mary, Florida, 2007.

Muldrow, Diane. *Everything I Need To Know I Learned From A Little Golden Book*. Golden Books, New York, New York, 2013.

Navajo, Jose Luis. *Mondays With My Old Pastor*. Thomas Nelson, Ic. Nashville, Tennessee, 2012.

Ricker, Michael. *A Heart A Flame*. Johnson Printing Company, Brandenton, Florida, 2004.

Rohr, Richard. *The Universal Christ*. Convergent Books, New York, New York, 2019.

Sapp, David, *There is a River.* 1969

Sifton, Elisabeth, *The Serenity Prayer: Faith and Politics in Times of War and Peace*. Norton, New York, 2004.

Schuller, Robert A. *Getting Through What You're Going Through*. Thomas Nelson, Inc. Nashville, Tennessee, 1986.

Schuller, Robert H. *Turning Hurts Into Halos and Scars Into Stars*. Thomas Nelson, Inc., Nashville, Tennessee, 1999.

Stanley, Dr. Charles. *Walking With God*. Thomas Nelson, Inc., Nashville, Tennessee, 2012.

Strobel, Lee. *The Case For Miracles*. Zondervan, Grand Rapids, Michigan, 2018.

Tanner, Dan. *A Collection Of Quotes Compiled by*. Unpublished, Blackshear, Georgia, 1999.

Willard, Dallas, *The Divine Conspiracy: Rediscovering Our Hidden Life In God*. HarperCollings Publishers, New York, New York, 1998.

Wommack, Andrew. *How To Find, Follow, Fulfill God's Will*. Harrison House Publishers, Tulsa, Oklahoma, 2013.

CPSIA information can be obtained
at www.ICGtesting.com
Printed in the USA
FSHW021903190620
71355FS